DEIN COACH ZUM ERFOLG!

So geht's ins ActiveBook:

Du kannst auf die Hördateien und alle digitalen Inhalte zu diesem Band online zugreifen. Registriere dich dazu unter **www.stark-verlag.de/mystark** mit deinem **persönlichen Zugangscode**:

93555ML-002215

gültig bis 31. Juli 2022

W0004721

Das ActiveBook bietet dir:

- Viele interaktive Übungsaufgaben zu prüfungsrelevanten Kompetenzen
- Tipps zur Bearbeitung der Aufgaben
- Sofortige Ergebnisauswertung und Feedback
- „MindCards" mit nützlichen Wendungen

ActiveBook

DEIN COACH ZUM ERFOLG!

So kannst du interaktiv lernen:

 Interaktive Aufgaben

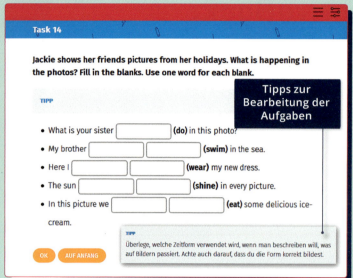

Tipps zur Bearbeitung der Aufgaben

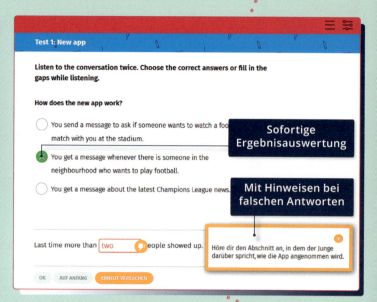

Sofortige Ergebnisauswertung

Mit Hinweisen bei falschen Antworten

 Web-App „MindCards"

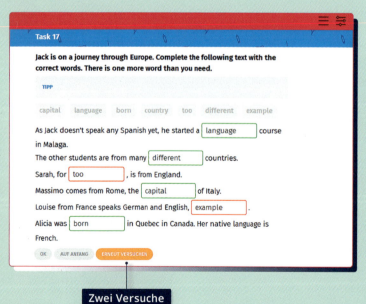

Zwei Versuche pro Aufgabe

Nützliche Wendungen mit Übersetzung

Individuelles Lernen nach dem Karteikartensystem

Systemvoraussetzungen:
- Windows 7/8/10 oder Mac OS X ab 10.9
- Mindestens 1024×768 Pixel Bildschirmauflösung
- Chrome, Firefox oder ähnlicher Webbrowser
- Internetzugang

 Speaking

 Writing

2022

Training Quali
Original-Prüfungsaufgaben

Bayern

Englisch

© 2021 Stark Verlag GmbH
16. neu bearbeitete und ergänzte Auflage
www.stark-verlag.de

Das Werk und alle seine Bestandteile sind urheberrechtlich geschützt. Jede vollständige oder teilweise Vervielfältigung, Verbreitung und Veröffentlichung bedarf der ausdrücklichen Genehmigung des Verlages. Dies gilt insbesondere für Vervielfältigungen, Mikroverfilmungen sowie die Speicherung und Verarbeitung in elektronischen Systemen.

Inhalt

Vorwort
Hinweise und Tipps zum Quali

Übungsaufgaben zu den Kompetenzbereichen

1	Kompetenzbereich: Hör- und Hörsehverstehen	1
1.1	Strategien zum Kompetenzbereich „Hör- und Hörsehverstehen" . . .	1
1.2	Übungsaufgaben zum Kompetenzbereich „Hör- und Hörsehverstehen"	3
	Test 1: In the supermarket	3
	Test 2: At the airport	4
	Test 3: Mrs Brown at the shoe store	6
	Test 4: Visit to Stirling Castle	7
2	Kompetenzbereich: Sprachgebrauch	10
2.1	Strategien zum Kompetenzbereich „Sprachgebrauch" ▶	10
2.2	Übungsaufgaben zum Kompetenzbereich „Sprachgebrauch"	11
3	Kompetenzbereich: Leseverstehen	24
3.1	Strategien zum Kompetenzbereich „Leseverstehen"	24
3.2	Übungsaufgaben zum Kompetenzbereich „Leseverstehen"	25
	Test 1: Treasure Hunting at the Florida Keys	25
	Test 2: Camels in Australia	28
	Test 3: Is autonomous driving becoming a reality?	31
	Test 4: Kelechi Iheanacho	34
4	Kompetenzbereich: Sprachmittlung	37
4.1	Strategien zum Kompetenzbereich „Sprachmittlung"	37
4.2	Übungsaufgaben zum Kompetenzbereich „Sprachmittlung"	38
	Test 1: Signs and posters	38
	Test 2: Wimbledon	42
	Test 3: Bungee jumping rules	44
	Test 4: Undara Lava Tubes	46
5	Kompetenzbereich: Text- und Medienkompetenzen	49
5.1	Strategien zum Kompetenzbereich „Text- und Medienkompetenzen"	49
5.2	Übungsaufgaben zum Kompetenzbereich „Text- und Medien- kompetenzen"	50
	Test 1: Bungee jumping in New Zealand	50
	Test 2: Puppies	52
	Test 3: Postcard from Kovalam	54
6	Kompetenzbereich: Schreiben	56
6.1	Strategien zum Kompetenzbereich „Schreiben"	56

Inhalt

6.2 Hilfreiche Wendungen zur Textproduktion 58

6.3 Übungsaufgaben zum Kompetenzbereich „Schreiben" 61

7   Kompetenzbereich: Sprechen 78

7.1 Hinweise und Strategien zum Kompetenzbereich „Sprechen" 78

7.2 Hilfreiche Wendungen und Beispiele zum Kompetenzbereich „Sprechen" 80

7.3 Übungsaufgaben zum Kompetenzbereich „Sprechen" 82

Anhang: Kurzgrammatik 93

Musteraufgabe und Original-Prüfungsaufgaben

Offizielle Musteraufgabe zum neuen Quali ab 2022

Hör- und Hörsehverstehen E-1

Sprachgebrauch E-3

Leseverstehen E-4

Sprachmittlung E-7

Text- und Medienkompetenzen E-9

Schreiben E-11

Abschlussprüfung 2014

Listening Comprehension .... E 2014-1

Use of English .... E 2014-2

Reading Comprehension .... E 2014-4

Text Production .... E 2014-7

Abschlussprüfung 2015

Listening Comprehension .... E 2015-1

Use of English .... E 2015-3

Reading Comprehension .... E 2015-5

Text Production .... E 2015-8

Abschlussprüfung 2016

Listening Comprehension .... E 2016-1

Use of English .... E 2016-3

Reading Comprehension .... E 2016-4

Text Production .... E 2016-7

Abschlussprüfung 2017

Listening Comprehension .... E 2017-1

Use of English .... E 2017-3

Reading Comprehension .... E 2017-5

Text Production .... E 2017-9

Abschlussprüfung 2018

Listening Comprehension .... E 2018-1

Use of English .... E 2018-3

Reading Comprehension .... E 2018-5

Text Production .... E 2018-9

Inhalt

Abschlussprüfung 2019
Listening Comprehension .... E 2019-1
Use of English .... E 2019-2
Reading Comprehension .... E 2019-4
Text Production .... E 2019-7

Abschlussprüfung 2020
Listening Comprehension .... E 2020-1
Use of English .... E 2020-2
Reading Comprehension .... E 2020-4
Text Production .... E 2020-7

Abschlussprüfung 2021 .... www.stark-verlag.de/mystark

Sobald die Original-Prüfungsaufgaben 2021 zur Veröffentlichung freigegeben sind, können sie als **PDF** auf der Plattform **MyStark** heruntergeladen werden (Zugangscode vgl. Farbseiten vorne im Buch).

Hördateien

Text 1: In the supermarket
Text 2: At the airport
Text 3: Mrs Brown at the shoe store
Text 4: Visit to Stirling Castle
Offizielle Musteraufgabe
Abschlussprüfung 2014
Abschlussprüfung 2015
Abschlussprüfung 2016
Abschlussprüfung 2017
Abschlussprüfung 2018
Abschlussprüfung 2019
Abschlussprüfung 2020
Abschlussprüfung 2021

Hinweis: Die Audio-Dateien befinden sich ebenfalls auf der Plattform **MyStark**, auf die du über den **Zugangscode** vorne im Buch gelangst.

Hörtexte Übungsaufgaben:
- gesprochen von Daniel Holzberg und Barbara Krzoska
- Soundeffekte: soundsnap, pacdv und freesound

Autorin: Birgit Mohr
Illustration Kurzgrammatik: Paul Jenkinson

Texte und Angaben der Original-Prüfungsaufgaben / Musteraufgaben:
© Bayerisches Staatsministerium für Unterricht und Kultus

Jeweils im Herbst erscheinen die neuen Ausgaben des Qualifizierenden Abschlusses der Mittelschule.
Sollten nach Erscheinen dieses Bandes noch wichtige Änderungen in der Abschlussprüfung vom Kultusministerium bekannt gegeben werden, findest du aktuelle Informationen dazu auf der Plattform MyStark.

Vorwort

Liebe Schülerin, lieber Schüler,

mit dem vorliegenden Buch kannst du dein Englisch dauerhaft verbessern und dich selbstständig und effektiv auf den **Quali** vorbereiten oder einfach nur sicherstellen, dass du dem Englischunterricht gut folgen kannst.

- Jedes Kapitel widmet sich einem **Fertigkeitsbereich** des Quali. Zu Beginn erfährst du jeweils, welche Anforderungen auf dich zukommen können und wie du dich am besten darauf vorbereitest. Du kannst also gezielt bestimmte Bereiche herausgreifen, die du dann besonders übst.
- Anhand der **Übungen** kannst du trainieren, wie man mit verschiedenen Aufgabenstellungen umgeht und wie man sie erfolgreich löst.
- In der **Kurzgrammatik** werden alle wichtigen grammatischen Themen knapp erläutert und an Beispielsätzen veranschaulicht.
- Am Ende des Buches findest du die **Original-Aufgaben der Abschlussprüfungen 2014 bis 2020**. Der Jahrgang **2021** erscheint in digitaler Form. Anhand der Original-Aufgaben und der offiziellen **Musteraufgabe zum neuen Quali ab 2022** kannst du deine Kenntnisse sozusagen „unter Prüfungsbedingungen" testen.
- Im **Lösungsband** (Best.-Nr.: 93554) findest du ausführliche Lösungsvorschläge mit vielen hilfreichen Hinweisen und Tipps zum Lösen der Aufgaben.

Digitale Zusätze:

- Neben vielen **Aufgaben** findest du das Symbol für „interaktive Aufgabe". Diese Aufgaben kannst du auch am Computer oder Tablet bearbeiten.
- Alle **Hörtexte** stehen dir als **MP3-Dateien** zur Verfügung.
- Mit der Web-App „**MindCards**" kannst du am Smartphone **hilfreiche Wendungen** zu den Kompetenzen „Schreiben" und „Sprechen" wiederholen. Über nebenstehende QR-Codes und unten stehende Links gelangst du zu den MindCards.
  https://www.stark-verlag.de/mindcards/writing-1
  https://www.stark-verlag.de/mindcards/speaking-1

Schreiben

Sprechen

Auf alle **digitalen Inhalte** zu deinem Band (Abschlussprüfung 2021, Hördateien, MindCards, Video und ActiveBook) kannst du online über die Plattform **MyStark** zugreifen. Verwende dazu deinen **persönlichen Zugangscode** vorne im Buch.

Viel Spaß beim Üben und viel Erfolg in der Prüfung!

Birgit Mohr

Hinweise und Tipps zum Quali

1   Ablauf der Prüfung

Am Ende der 9. Klasse kannst du in verschiedenen Fächern an einer besonderen Leistungsfeststellung teilnehmen, um zusätzlich zum „erfolgreichen Abschluss der Mittelschule" den „Qualifizierenden Abschluss der Mittelschule" zu erwerben. An dieser Leistungsfeststellung können auch externe Bewerber einer anderen Schulart teilnehmen.

Die Leistungsfeststellung im Fach Englisch besteht sowohl aus einer **schriftlichen** als auch aus einer **mündlichen Prüfung**. Nur der schriftliche Teil der Prüfung ist zentral gestellt und ist somit für alle Schüler*innen in Bayern gleich. Der mündliche Teil wird von Lehrkräften der Schule, an der du die Prüfung ablegst, ausgearbeitet und kann von Schule zu Schule verschieden sein. Besonders für externe Teilnehmer*innen ist es wichtig, sich rechtzeitig an der zuständigen Schule über die genauen Prüfungsanforderungen zu informieren. Setze dich auch im Fall einer anerkannten Rechtschreibstörung mit deiner Schule in Verbindung und erkundige dich über einen möglichen Nachteilsausgleich.

Erlaubte Hilfsmittel: In der schriftlichen Prüfung darfst du ab dem Quali 2022 in allen Teilen ein zweisprachiges Wörterbuch in Printform verwenden – digitale Übersetzungshilfen sind nicht erlaubt. Über zugelassene Hilfsmittel in der mündlichen Prüfung entscheidet die Prüfungskommission der jeweiligen Schule. Erkundige dich rechtzeitig bei deiner Fachlehrkraft, wie die Bedingungen an deiner Schule genau aussehen.

2   Inhalte

Die Leistungsfeststellung im Fach Englisch setzt sich aus den folgenden Teilen zusammen: Die zentral gestellte **schriftliche Prüfung** und die **mündliche Prüfung**, die von der Schule organisiert wird. Die schriftliche Prüfung ab dem Quali 2022 besteht aus folgenden Kompetenzbereichen:

A Hör- und Hörsehverstehen
B Sprachgebrauch
C Leseverstehen
D Sprachmittlung (Englisch – Deutsch)
E Text- und Medienkompetenzen
F Schreiben

Die Arbeitszeit beträgt insgesamt 120 Minuten.

Die Gesamtpunktzahl von 92 Punkten setzt sich folgendermaßen zusammen:
Teile A, B, C: jeweils 18 Punkte
Teile D und E: jeweils 9 Punkte
Teil F: 20 Punkte
Es können auch halbe Punkte vergeben werden.

Hinweise und Tipps zum Quali

3 Leistungsanforderungen

Schriftliche Prüfung

In der Prüfung gibt es meist ein Rahmenthema (z. B. Umwelt, ein englischsprachiges Land oder eine Region), das in jedem Prüfungsteil behandelt wird. Folgende Kompetenzen werden geprüft:

Hör- und Hörsehverstehen: Du hörst mehrere Texte (z. B. Gespräche), auf die jeweils Aufgaben folgen, die überprüfen, ob du das Gehörte verstanden hast. Dabei musst du z. B. entscheiden, ob eine Aussage über den gehörten Text richtig oder falsch ist *(true/false)* oder dir wird ein Lückentext vorgelegt, den du vervollständigen sollst *(fill-in)*. Auch kann es sein, dass du auf Fragen in Stichpunkten antworten *(short answers)* oder das korrekte Ende eines Satzes ankreuzen musst *(multiple choice)*.

Sprachgebrauch: In diesem Teil werden dein Wortschatz, deine Grammatikkenntnisse und deine Ausdrucksfähigkeit getestet. Diese Fähigkeiten werden z. B. mit Lückentexten überprüft, in die du die richtigen Wörter einsetzen musst, oder bei denen du Wörter einer Wortfamilie in die richtige Form bringen sollst. Außerdem können dir hier fehlerhafte Sätze zur Verbesserung vorgelegt werden.

Leseverstehen: Anhand von Aufgaben zu einem Lesetext wird hier dein Leseverständnis überprüft. So musst du z. B. Fragen zum Text in kurzen Sätzen oder Stichworten beantworten *(short answers)*, richtige Statements erkennen oder zu einer Aussage die korrekte Antwort ankreuzen *(multiple choice)*.

Sprachmittlung: Grundlage für die Sprachmittlung bilden englischsprachige Texte, z. B. ein Internet-Blog oder eine Seite aus einem Reiseführer. Je nach Aufgabenstellung entnimmst du diesen Texten bestimmte Informationen, die du anschließend in deinen eigenen Worten auf Deutsch wiedergibst, z. B. in einer E-Mail, als Plakat oder als Textnachricht.

Text- und Medienkompetenzen: In diesem Prüfungsteil findest du englischsprachige Textvorlagen, wie etwa einen Tagebucheintrag, einen Chatverlauf oder ein Kochrezept. Du entnimmst diesen Texten je nach Aufgabenstellung bestimmte Informationen und verwendest diese, um z. B. einen Lebenslauf oder ein Formular auf Englisch zu ergänzen oder einen Brief zu beantworten.

Schreiben: Du kannst hier zwischen dem Schreiben einer *Correspondence* (E-Mail, Brief, Bewerbung) und dem *Creative Writing* (Bildergeschichte oder Bild mit Impulsen) wählen. In beiden Fällen findest du Vorgaben zu Form und Inhalt, die du beim Verfassen deines Textes berücksichtigen sollst.

Mündliche Prüfung

Die mündliche Prüfung dauert insgesamt **15 Minuten**. Sie kann von mehreren Schülern gleichzeitig absolviert werden. Sie enthält in der Regel folgende Prüfungsformate:

▶ *Picture-based interview:* Gespräch auf Grundlage eines Bildes
▶ *Topic-based talk:* Zusammenhängendes Sprechen mittels inhaltlicher Impulse
▶ *Interpreting/Mediation* (Sprachmittlung)*:* Dolmetschen in Alltagssituationen

Hinweise und Tipps zum Quali

4 Methodische Hinweise und allgemeine Tipps zur Prüfung

Vorbereitung

▶ Bereite dich **langfristig** vor. Dieses Buch enthält Aufgaben zu allen **Fertigkeitsbereichen** der neuen Prüfung. Du kannst sie anhand der **Übungsaufgaben** und der **Musteraufgabe** in diesem Buch sehr gut trainieren. Auch die alten **Originalprüfungen** eignen sich weiterhin ideal zur Vorbereitung, da die Bereiche „Hörverstehen" (früher: *Listening Comprehension*), „Sprachgebrauch" (*Use of English*), „Leseverstehen" (*Reading Comprehension*) und „Schreiben" (*Text Production*) gleich geblieben sind.

▶ Übe unter möglichst „echten" **Prüfungsbedingungen:** Versuche, die Aufgaben in der **vorgegebenen Zeit** zu schaffen. Wenn du sie zunächst nicht in dieser Zeit lösen kannst, solltest du sie in regelmäßigen Abständen wiederholen, bis du sicherer und schneller wirst. Versuche stets, alle Aufgaben **selbstständig** zu lösen. Solltest du einmal gar nicht weiterkommen, kann ein Blick in die Lösung (im separaten Lösungsband) hilfreich sein, da dort nützliche **Hinweise und Tipps** zur Bearbeitung der Aufgaben gegeben werden. Vergleiche zum Schluss deine Lösung mit der Beispiellösung und suche gegebenenfalls nach Grammatik- und Rechtschreibfehlern.

In der Prüfung

Schriftliche Prüfung

▶ **Lies** die Aufgabenstellung **genau** durch.

▶ Achte darauf, auf welchen **Kompetenzbereich** sich die Aufgabe bezieht. Welche **Methoden** (z. B. Unterstreichen von wichtigen Textstellen) kennst du für diesen Bereich?

Mündliche Prüfung

▶ Befolge die **Anweisungen** und reagiere auf **Anregungen**.

▶ Versuche, möglichst **umfangreiche** Antworten zu geben und das Gespräch „am Laufen" zu halten.

5 Bewertung

Die **Gesamtnote im Fach Englisch** wird folgendermaßen berechnet:

Die Summe aus 2 × Jahresfortgang + 1 × Note in der schriftlichen Prüfung + 1 × Note in der mündlichen Prüfung wird durch 4 geteilt.

Die Bewertung deiner schriftlichen und mündlichen Leistung erfolgt durch **zwei Lehrkräfte**. Die Noten, die du im schriftlichen und mündlichen Teil erzielst, werden 1:1 gewichtet, zählen also **gleich viel**. Für die **schriftliche** Prüfung im Fach Englisch gilt eine einheitliche Zuordnung von erreichter Punktzahl und Note, die für alle bayerischen Schulen **verbindlich** ist. In der **mündlichen Prüfung** erfolgt die Notenvergabe nach **schulinternen** Maßstäben. Den Qualifizierenden Abschluss der Mittelschule hast du erlangt, wenn dein Schnitt aus der Summe aller Jahres- und Quali-Noten 3,0 oder besser ist.

▶ **Übungsaufgaben zu den Kompetenzbereichen**

Bildnachweis: © 123rf.com

1 Kompetenzbereich: Hör- und Hörsehverstehen

Hörverstehenstexte und die zugehörigen Aufgabenstellungen können sehr unterschiedlich sein. Die Texte, die du im Unterricht oder im Rahmen von Proben oder im Quali zu hören bekommst, spiegeln meist **reale Sprechsituationen** wider, d. h. man kann solche oder ähnliche Texte im wirklichen Leben hören. Die Inhalte der Texte können von der Begrüßungsansprache eines Flugkapitäns über die Lautsprecheransagen an einem Bahnhof oder die Kommentierung eines Fußballspiels bis hin zu Gesprächen zwischen mehreren Personen reichen. Genauso vielfältig wie die verschiedenen Arten von Hörtexten können auch die Aufgabenstellungen ausfallen. In diesem Kapitel werden dir die häufigsten Textarten und Aufgabenstellungen zum Kompetenzbereich „Hör- und Hörsehverstehen" vorgestellt.

1.1 Strategien zum Kompetenzbereich „Hör- und Hörsehverstehen"

Vorgehen beim Üben

Zu Übungszwecken kannst du dir den Hörverstehenstext ruhig so oft anhören, wie du möchtest. Lies ihn aber nicht durch, sondern versuche, die Arbeitsaufträge nur durch Zuhören zu bearbeiten. Lies den Hörverstehenstext im Lösungsheft nur dann, wenn du überhaupt nicht auf die richtige Lösung kommst. Bei der Bearbeitung der Hörverstehensaufgaben solltest du wie folgt vorgehen:

▶ Höre dir den entsprechenden Text einmal an, sodass du weißt, worum es darin geht.

▶ Lies die Aufgabenstellungen genau durch. Hast du sie alle verstanden? Kläre unbekannte Wörter mithilfe eines Wörterbuchs.

▶ Höre dir den Text noch einmal an. Diesen Schritt kannst du so oft wiederholen, wie es für dich hilfreich ist.

▶ Höre dir den Text an und versuche dabei, die Aufgaben zu lösen.

▶ Wenn du alle Aufgaben bearbeitet hast, solltest du die Richtigkeit deiner Lösungen überprüfen, indem du dir den Text ein weiteres Mal anhörst.

▶ Anschließend überprüfst du deine Antworten anhand der Lösungen im Lösungsheft. Wenn du viele Fehler gemacht hast, dann überlege genau, wie sie zustande gekommen sind. Hast du den Hörtext nicht richtig verstanden? Hast du die Fragestellung falsch verstanden? Lies gegebenenfalls den Hörverstehenstext durch und wiederhole die gesamte Aufgabe in ein paar Tagen.

▶ Versuche, mit der Bearbeitung jeder weiteren Hörverstehensaufgabe in diesem Buch die Zahl der Hörsequenzen zu reduzieren, bis du bei der im Quali üblichen Anzahl angelangt bist.

Kompetenzbereich: Hör- und Hörsehverstehen

Vorgehen in Prüfungssituationen

In einer Probe oder später im Quali hörst du den **Hörverstehenstext meist zweimal**. Er wird dir in der Regel von einer CD vorgespielt.

Arbeitsschritt 1

Nach dem ersten Vorspielen bzw. Vorlesen des Textes wird meist eine **kurze Pause** gemacht, in der du dir die **Aufgabenstellungen** auf dem Arbeitsblatt noch einmal **ansehen** darfst. Lies dabei die Aufgabenstellungen ganz sorgfältig durch und überlege genau, welche Informationen du bislang noch nicht verstanden hast. Auf sie musst du beim zweiten Hören besonders achten. Zu den Aufgaben, die du nach dem ersten Hören bereits beantworten kannst, kannst du gleich die **richtige Lösung aufschreiben**.

Arbeitsschritt 2

Wenn überhaupt, dann solltest du dir erst während des zweiten Hördurchgangs **Notizen machen**. Das Anfertigen von Notizen kann dich vom Zuhören abhalten, daher solltest du dabei ganz gezielt vorgehen und wirklich nur die wichtigsten Dinge aufschreiben, die du dir nicht im Kopf merken kannst. Da du nach dem ersten Hören die Arbeitsaufträge lesen konntest, weißt du, welche **Detailinformationen** gefragt sind. Solche Detailinformationen können beispielsweise Adressen sein oder es werden Eigennamen buchstabiert, die du zur Lösung einer Aufgabe exakt aufschreiben musst. In solchen Fällen lohnt es sich, Notizen zu machen.

Arbeitsschritt 3

Nach dem zweiten Hören hast du in der Regel genügend Zeit, um jede Aufgabe auf deinem Arbeitsblatt noch einmal gründlich durchzulesen und entsprechend zu lösen. Hast du nach dem ersten Hören bereits einige Aufgaben beantwortet, so überprüfe sie jetzt noch einmal auf ihre Richtigkeit. Bei Detailinformationen, die innerhalb von einzelnen Aufgaben gefragt sind, solltest du zur Beantwortung deine Notizen heranziehen.

Einen Punkt solltest du immer beachten: Die Fragen folgen in der Regel der Reihenfolge im Text, d. h. wenn du die Lösung zu einer der mittleren Fragen nicht weißt, dann passe beim zweiten Hören besonders gut in der Mitte des Textes auf.

TIPP

- Höre genau zu. Worum geht es im Text?
- Nach dem ersten Hören: Lies die Aufgabenstellungen nochmals genau durch. Bearbeite die Aufgaben, zu denen du schon die Lösung weißt. Welche Informationen fehlen dir noch?
- Mache dir während des zweiten Hörens Notizen über Details, die du für die Beantwortung der Fragen noch brauchst.
- Nach dem zweiten Hören: Löse nun die restlichen Aufgaben. Überprüfe auch noch einmal die Aufgaben, die du nach dem ersten Hören bereits gelöst hast.

Kompetenzbereich: Hör- und Hörsehverstehen

1.2 Übungsaufgaben zum Kompetenzbereich „Hör- und Hörsehverstehen"

Test 1: In the supermarket

Wortschatz: bargain – *günstiges Angebot, Schnäppchen*; selection: *Auswahl*

Listen to the loudspeaker announcement in the supermarket.

> **Multiple choice**
> Hier wird dir eine Frage oder ein Satzanfang mit mehreren möglichen Antworten bzw. Alternativen vorgegeben und du musst entscheiden, welche Alternative zum Inhalt des Textes passt. Dabei musst du z. B. ein Kästchen ankreuzen oder das richtige Wort unterstreichen.

TIPP

1. a) Tick (✓) the correct answer. The name of the supermarket is …
   - ☐ Richie's.
   - ☐ Redmond's.
   - ☐ Ladies.
   - ☐ Ready's.

   b) What is the supermarket celebrating this week? Tick (✓) the correct answer.
   - ☐ Summer sale
   - ☐ Fruit week
   - ☐ Health week
   - ☐ Beauty week

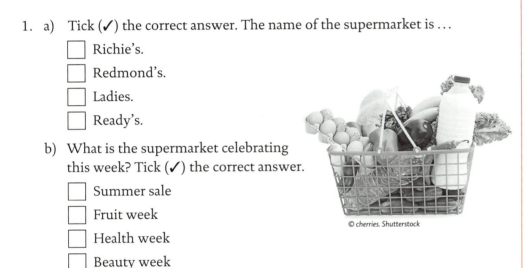
© cherries. Shutterstock

2. Fill in the correct numbers. How much do these goods cost?

   a) One kilo of apples costs _____ pence.
   b) One 5 kg bag of potatoes costs _____ pound(s) _____ pence.
   c) Every natural bath product costs _____ pence.
   d) The sun lotions cost _____ % less than normal.

13. Each of the following sentences contains one word which is wrong. Cross it out and fill in the correct word.

    a) The supermarket offers you the best health protests at the best prices you can find. Correct word: _____
    b) You can find apples, pears and tomatoes in the friend and vegetable department. Correct word: _____
    c) In the cosmetics department, you will find a wide selection of normal bath products. Correct word: _____
    d) Take your money to find out about our offers. Correct word: _____

Test 2: At the airport

Wortschatz: aisle – *Gang*

TIPP

True or false
Bei diesem Aufgabentyp sollst du jeweils entscheiden, ob eine Aussage richtig oder falsch ist. Meist weicht dabei die Formulierung der Aussage in der Aufgabenstellung etwas von der im Text ab.

Part 1

1. Listen to the dialogue and tick (✓) the correct answer.

	true	false
a) The Millers want to fly to Munich.	☐	☐
b) They forgot their tickets.	☐	☐
c) They will sit by the window.	☐	☐
d) They have luggage which they have to check in.	☐	☐

2. Tick (✓) the correct answer for each question.

a) What does the woman at the service desk ask Mr Miller to give her?

☐ their tickets

☐ their tickets and passports

☐ their boarding cards

b) Where do the Millers have to change planes?

☐ in France

☐ in Frankfurt

☐ in Munich

c) When does the plane take off?

☐ in 30 minutes

☐ in 12 minutes

☐ in 20 minutes

© Brian Kinney. Shutterstock

d) What is the number of the gate Mr and Mrs Miller have to go to?

17	70	7
☐	☐	☐

Kompetenzbereich: Hör- und Hörsehverstehen | 5

Part 2

13. Who said it? Fill in the correct letters (A, B or C).

A
© racorn. Shutterstock

B
© Ana Bokan. Shutterstock

C
© Andres Rodriguez/123rf.com

a) "You are sitting in my seat." _____

b) "It must be the airline's mistake." _____

c) "The flight number and date are correct." _____

d) "This boarding card is for another flight." _____

e) "I can't find my boarding card." _____

14. Fill in the missing information.

Boarding the plane	
a) Seat number on the woman's boarding card:	_____
b) What Mr Miller is asked to show:	_____
c) The last time the woman travelled to Frankfurt:	_____
d) Where the flight attendant is going to look up the correct seat:	_____

© 06photo. Shutterstock

Test 3: Mrs Brown at the shoe store

Wortschatz:
aisle – *Gang*
casual shoes – *Freizeitschuhe*
loafers – *Halbschuhe*
tight – *eng*

Part 1

1. Underline the correct words.

   a) Mrs Brown is looking for a pair of shoes for **autumn/summer/sports**.

   b) Mrs Brown would like to have **cheap/elegant/comfortable** shoes.

   c) The shoes that Mrs Brown is looking for should be **grey/brown/beige**.

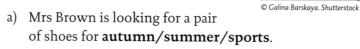
© Galina Barskaya. Shutterstock

Part 2

2. Find the correct ending to each sentence:

   a) Mrs Brown does not want to have shoes that are open at the tip so that it is not possible to see her _____. (legs/toes/nose/heels)

   b) She would like to have shoes which can be worn with _____. (a dress/trousers/socks/stockings)

   c) Mrs Brown chooses to try shoes which are from _____. (Italy/England/France/Germany)

Part 3

3. Complete each sentence.

   a) The first pair of shoes that Mrs Brown tries don't _____.

   b) Instead, she would like to try size _____.

   c) The shoes that Mrs Brown buys are size _____.

Part 4

4. True or false? Tick (✓) the correct answer.

	true	false
a) At the cash register, Mrs Brown pays for a pair of beige shoes.	☐	☐
b) The shoes cost £ 69.95.	☐	☐
c) Mrs Brown pays with her credit card.	☐	☐

Kompetenzbereich: Hör- und Hörsehverstehen | 7

Test 4: Visit to Stirling Castle

Part 1

1. Tabby and Nick are talking about Stirling Castle. Listen and tick (✓) the correct endings.

   a) Stirling Castle is the most important castle in ...

   ☐ Wales.
   ☐ Ireland.
   ☐ England.
   ☐ Scotland.

   b) Mary, Queen of Scots, and Mary Stuart were ...

   ☐ sisters.
   ☐ cousins.
   ☐ the same person.
   ☐ mother and daughter.

   c) When Mary, Queen of Scots, was crowned, she ...

   ☐ was still a baby.
   ☐ had her baby with her.
   ☐ didn't live at Stirling Castle.
   ☐ was already married.

   d) The ghost wearing a traditional Scottish costume is called ...

   ☐ "Stirling Ghost".
   ☐ "Highland Ghost".
   ☐ "Bagpipe Ghost".
   ☐ "Mary Stuart's Ghost".

   e) The "Green Lady" lost her life because she ...

   ☐ couldn't save the queen's life.
   ☐ was sleeping when a curtain caught fire.
   ☐ was badly injured when saving the queen's life.
   ☐ was shocked by the "Highland Ghost".

   f) The "Green Lady" was named after the colour of her ...

   ☐ face.
   ☐ hair.
   ☐ eyes.
   ☐ clothes.

Kompetenzbereich: Hör- und Hörsehverstehen

Part 2

2. Tabby and Nick are on a tour through Stirling Castle. Listen to the guide and answer the questions. Write short answers. One example is already given.

   Example: What architectural style is Stirling Castle?

   (It's) Renaissance.

   a) When was the palace of Stirling Castle built?
   _____

   b) In which year did the royal court leave the palace of Stirling Castle?
   _____

   c) Where did King James VI and the royal court move?
   _____

   d) How much did the renovation of the palace of Stirling Castle cost?
   _____

   e) Who made the paintings and furniture in the palace look like in Mary Stuart's time?
   _____

   f) The costumed characters demonstrate to visitors what life was like in which century?
   _____

Part 3

3. Tabby and Nick are wandering around Stirling Castle to find some costumed characters. Listen to the dialogue. Five of the following statements are true. Write the letters in the box. There is one example at the beginning (0).

   A Nick and Tabby are on their own.
   B Nick and Tabby didn't leave the tour.
   C Nick spotted a costumed character.
   D The costumed character was female.
   E The servant wasn't carrying anything.
   F Tabby saw the servant disappear into a wall.
   G The servant wore a green dress.
   H Tabby and Nick followed the servant.
   I Tabby and Nick decided to leave the place.

0	1	2	3	4
A				

© Can Stock Photo/iofoto

Kompetenzbereich: Hör- und Hörsehverstehen 9

Part 4

4. Tabby and Nick are back in the car. Listen to the dialogue. There is one mistake in each sentence. While listening cross out the word which is wrong and write down the correct one. One example is already given.

   a) "You are such an ~~idiom~~!"
      idiot

   b) "I'll never teach you anything about any place we visit, ever again."
      _____

   c) "Sorry, it was not so funny … you should have seen your face."
      _____

   d) "For a moment I really trusted you and thought there was a ghost!"
      _____

   e) "I swear I will never go into any palace with you again!"
      _____

© Foto: Finlay McWalter, CC BY-SA 3.0

2 Kompetenzbereich: Sprachgebrauch

Die Aufgabenstellungen, die dir im Unterricht oder in Proben und im Quali zum Bereich „Sprachgebrauch" begegnen, sind sehr vielfältig. Ziel dieser Aufgaben ist es, deinen Wortschatz und deine Grammatikkenntnisse zu testen.

2.1 Strategien zum Kompetenzbereich „Sprachgebrauch"

Um im Bereich „Sprachgebrauch" gut abzuschneiden, ist es wichtig, dass du intensiv übst. Je mehr Wörter du in der Fremdsprache kennst und in Gesprächen oder beim Schreiben anwenden kannst, desto treffender und abwechslungsreicher kannst du dich ausdrücken. Es gibt verschiedene Methoden, um den Wortschatz zu erweitern.

2.1.1 Wortschatz

Natürlich kannst du mit den Vokabellisten in deinem Englischbuch lernen. Zum Lernen deckst du dann jeweils eine Spalte ab. Du kannst dir auch **Vokabeln auf Karteikarten** notieren. Schreibe den englischen Begriff auf die Vorderseite der Karte. Notiere dazu auch einen englischen Satz, in dem das Wort vorkommt. So lernst du gleich, in welchem Zusammenhang das Wort gebraucht wird. Notiere auch sonst alles, was zu der Vokabel gehört (z. B. bei Verben nicht nur den Infinitiv, sondern auch die verschiedenen Personalformen „I …, you …, he/she/it …" oder die Präpositionen, die nach bestimmten Verben stehen, wie z. B. „to look at sb/sth"). Auf die Rückseite der Karteikarte schreibst du die deutsche Übersetzung des Wortes.

Welche Methode du auch anwendest oder mit anderen Strategien kombinierst, lerne nie zu viele Vokabeln auf einmal! Am besten ist es, wenn du neue Vokabeln immer in kleinen Gruppen von sechs bis sieben Wörtern lernst. Lies sie dir zunächst einige Male durch, wiederhole sie auch laut – in einer Fremdsprache kommt es auch auf die korrekte Aussprache an – und lege sie dann für etwa 20 Minuten zur Seite. Dann fängst du von vorne an. Diese Pausen sind wichtig, damit sich das gerade Gelernte setzen kann. So fällt es dir nicht schwer, dir bald einen umfangreichen englischen Wortschatz anzueignen.

  Eine Übersicht zu verschiedenen Methoden des Vokabellernens gibt dir auch ein **Video**, zu dem du über nebenstehenden QR-Code gelangst.

2.1.2 Grammatik

Im Quali wird der gesamte englische Grammatikstoff geprüft, den du dir über mehrere Schuljahre hinweg angeeignet hast. In der Prüfung sind die Aufgaben üblicherweise nicht nach grammatikalischen Themen geordnet, sondern es werden in einer Aufgabe verschiedene Themen, z. B. die Zeiten, Steigerungsformen oder *if*-Sätze getestet. Um dich schrittweise darauf vorzubereiten, findest du im folgenden Teil viele Aufgaben, die sich auf jeweils nur *einen* Grammatikbereich beschränken. Somit hast du die Möglichkeit herauszufinden, welche Themen du beherrschst bzw. welche du nochmals üben solltest. In der Kurzgrammatik in diesem Band kannst du die wichtigsten Themen noch einmal wiederholen.

2.1.3 Sprechanlässe

Um eine Situation kommunikativ erfolgreich zu bewältigen, musst du die an dich gerichteten Informationen verstehen, um dich verständigen zu können. Dies wird dir am besten gelingen, wenn du dir neben einem guten Wortschatz auch solide Grammatikkenntnisse angeeignet hast. Nur so wirst du z. B. deinem Gesprächspartner klarmachen können, ob du über ein zurückliegendes oder ein zukünftiges Ereignis berichtest. Auch in einem nicht-englischsprachigem Umfeld kannst du nach Möglichkeiten suchen, mit dem Englischen in Kontakt zu kommen. Du kannst eine englischsprachige Lektüre lesen, englische Websites besuchen, oder einen dir bekannten Film bzw. eine Serie auf Englisch ansehen, indem du „Englisch" als Sprache wählst.

2.2 Übungsaufgaben zum Kompetenzbereich „Sprachgebrauch"

Hier findest du zahlreiche Aufgaben zum Überprüfen und Erweitern deines Wortschatzes und deiner Grammatikkenntnisse.

1. Read the sentences. Find two more words for each sentence.

   a) At school you find chalk, _Blackboard_ and _chairs_, for example.

   b) When it is cold in winter there is _snow_ and _____.

   c) In the zoo there are a lot of animals, for example monkeys, _____ and _____.

2. Find four words that fit the collective nouns "furniture" and "weather".

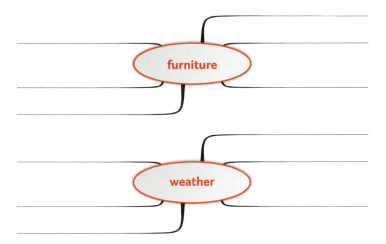

Kompetenzbereich: Sprachgebrauch

3. Find collective nouns for the following words/pictures.
   Example: juice, mineral water, lemonade: ___drinks___
   a) green, yellow, blue: colour
   b) _____

   v.l.n.r.: © Rob Wilson. Shutterstock, © wacpan.
   Shutterstock, © vladimiroquai. 123rf.com

   c) English, Dutch, French: _____

4. Find the word that does not go together with the others in the list.
   Example: **fruit:** banana, cherry, ~~potato~~, apple
   a) **vegetables:** tomato, onion, pineapple, beans
   b) **vehicles:** car, horse, bus, bike
   c) **drinks:** water, vinegar, juice, tea
   d) **meals:** breakfast, dinner, fork, lunch
   e) **flavours:** sweet, sour, soft, salty

   © robynmac. 123rf.com

5. Cross out the word which is wrong and find the collective noun.
   Example: banana, cherry, ~~potato~~, apple: → ___fruit___
   a) shirt, jeans, skirt, bag, pullover: → _____
   b) wheel, petrol, engine, pen, window screen: → _____
   c) arms, legs, food, eyes, hands: → _____
   d) potatoes, peas, carrots, beans, knife: → _____
   e) ice-cream, cake, pudding, meat, sweets: → _____

6. Where can you find them?
   Example: teacher, pupil, blackboard, chalk → ___school___
   a) menu, waiter, drinks → _____
   b) actors, seats, curtain → _____
   c) doctor, nurse, patient → _____
   d) priest, candles, prayer books → _____
   e) trees, dogs, bench → _____

© 123rf.com

Kompetenzbereich: Sprachgebrauch 13

7. In the following list there are seven words that sound the same as seven other words in the list. Match the words that sound the same.

> board • whole • no • break • hole • hour • piece • see • bored •
> know • sea • brake • peace • our

_____ – _____

_____ – _____

_____ – _____

_____ – _____

_____ – _____

_____ – _____

_____ – _____

8. Underline the word that fits.
Example: I **arrived** • **arrested** • **attended** late at school yesterday morning.

 a) It was dark **at** • **in** • **over** the morning when I went to school.

 b) The plane was **left** • **late** • **soon** this morning.

 c) I often **drive** • **go** • **miss** by train.

 d) **What** • **Which** • **Where** can I buy a watch, please?

9. Find the opposites of the following words.

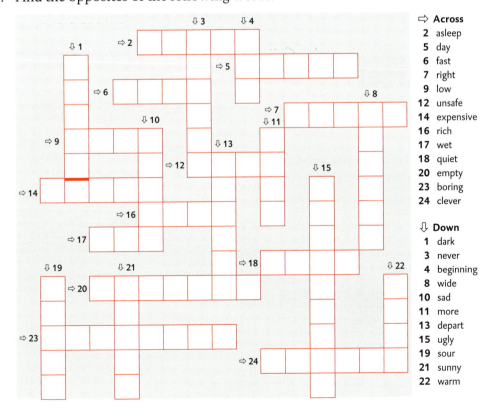

⇨ **Across**
2 asleep
5 day
6 fast
7 right
9 low
12 unsafe
14 expensive
16 rich
17 wet
18 quiet
20 empty
23 boring
24 clever

⇩ **Down**
1 dark
3 never
4 beginning
8 wide
10 sad
11 more
13 depart
15 ugly
19 sour
21 sunny
22 warm

Kompetenzbereich: Sprachgebrauch

10. Write down the feminine forms.
    a) policeman → _____
    b) prince → _____
    c) actor → _____
    d) waiter → _____

11. Find the correct plural forms for the following words.
    a) knife → _____
    b) mouse → _____
    c) man → _____
    d) woman → _____
    e) child → _____
    f) fish → _____
    g) leaf → _____
    h) tooth → _____

12. What's the word for …?
    a) the place where trains arrive and leave.
       - railway station ☐
       - airport ☐
       - parking lot ☐
    b) the place where you can book a holiday.
       - bakery ☐
       - travel agency ☐
       - plane ☐
    c) the thing you put your clothes in before you go on a trip.
       - box ☐
       - suitcase ☐
       - schoolbag ☐
    d) the document you need to prove your identity.
       - credit card ☐
       - bus ticket ☐
       - passport ☐

Kompetenzbereich: Sprachgebrauch | 15

13. What do you need …

a) to listen to the latest news?
- a telephone ☐
- a newspaper ☐
- a radio ☐

b) to write on paper?
- a pen ☐
- water colour ☐
- a mouse ☐

c) to tell your friend that you can't come to the date?
- a mailbox ☐
- a mobile phone ☐
- an envelope ☐

d) to open the door?
- a fork ☐
- a hammer ☐
- a key ☐

TIPP

Lückentexte
In der Prüfung wird oft auch anhand von Lückentexten oder einzelnen Lückensätzen geprüft, wie groß dein Wortschatz ist bzw. wie gut deine Grammatikkenntnisse sind. Die folgenden Arten von Lückentexten kommen am häufigsten vor:

– Der jeweilige **Anfangsbuchstabe** ist bereits vorgegeben:
 Beispiel: It is very hot and s_____ today. → sunny

– Es werden **Wörter** bereits **vorgegeben**, die du dann in die richtigen Lücken setzen musst, sodass der jeweilige Satz einen Sinn ergibt.

– Hinter der Lücke steht **in Klammern** das **Wort**, das in der richtigen oder in passender Form eingesetzt werden muss. Diese Variante findest du häufig bei Aufgaben, die deine Grammatikkenntnisse testen.
 Beispiel: Jessie _____ (be) in England last year. → was

 Auch im folgenden Beispiel ist ein Wort vorgegeben, das so verändert werden muss, dass es in den Satz passt. Hier musst du die Wortart anpassen bzw. du brauchst ein anderes Wort aus der Wortfamilie. Wenn z. B. ein Verb vorgegeben ist, in dem Satz jedoch ein Nomen fehlt, musst du dir überlegen, wie das Nomen zu dem vorgegebenen Verb lautet:
 Beispiel: Jessie's _____ (FLY) to London was late. → flight

– Manchmal gibt es auch gar **keine Vorgaben** und du musst selbst überlegen, welches Wort oder welcher Satz (z. B. bei Dialogen) in der Lücke einen Sinn ergibt.
 Beispiel:
 Jack: "_____?" → How are you
 Jessie: "Fine, thanks".

Prüfe immer, nachdem du die Lücken gefüllt hast, ob deine Lösungen im Satz einen Sinn ergeben! Sonst musst du deine Lösung noch einmal überdenken.

Kompetenzbereich: Sprachgebrauch

14. Complete the gaps in the following sentences.

a) Big Ben is a tourist **a**_____ in London.

b) The "Anne Frank House" is in Amsterdam. That is in the Netherlands. The people there are called the **D**_____.

c) The Leaning Tower of Pisa is in Italy. The people there **s**_____ Italian.

d) The Eiffel Tower is in Paris. Paris is the **c**_____ of France.

e) The Puerta del Sol is in Madrid, in Spain. People from Spain are called **S**_____.

15. At the new school. Fill in the gaps using the words in brackets in the correct form. Do not change the text.

a) Where is the cafeteria? – It's in the main _____ (BUILD).

b) Do you like the food there? – Yes, it's _____ (SURPRISE) good.

c) Who is that _____ (BEAUTY) girl over there? – That's my sister.

d) Why is she looking so _____ (SADNESS)? – Her _____ (FRIENDLY) Lili just moved away.

e) Where did she _____ (MOVEMENT)? – Back to _____ (FRENCH).

16. Clara calls her brother. Fill in the gaps with suitable words.

a) **Clara:** Hi Eric, how _____ you?

b) **Eric:** _____, thanks. How are you?

c) **Clara:** I'm fine, too. But I _____ you all.

d) **Eric:** We miss you, too. _____ are you coming home?

e) **Clara:** _____ Friday.

f) **Eric:** We're looking forward _____ seeing you.

17. Choose the correct verbs:

think • enjoy • hope • wear • forget • want • see

Tom is thinking about his performance in the school drama group:
"I'm going to _____ my suit and I _____ I will be very nervous. I _____ I won't _____ my lines. Even my grandparents _____ to come and _____ me acting. I hope everyone will _____ the evening."

Kompetenzbereich: Sprachgebrauch | 17

18. Fill in the missing parts from the box. You don't need all the words given.

> What • easy • to come • nice • plans • it's • to • crowded with tourists • where •
> will • week • forward • alright • to show you • shopping • sightseeing • empty

Sara: "Lisa and I are going ___to___ Paris on 12th May."

Pierre: "When _____ you arrive in Paris?"

Sara: "At 2.35 pm."

Pierre: "_____ is the name of the hotel you're staying at?"

Sara: "_____ Hôtel de Paris."

Pierre: "Do you have any _____ for your stay?"

Sara: "I want to do some _____ and visit the Eiffel Tower and the Champs-Elysées.

Pierre: "I would like _____ the nightlife in Paris. I'm looking _____ to seeing you next _____."

19. Fill in the correct prepositions from the box.
    There are more prepositions than you need.

    a) The teacher is sitting _____ the table.

    b) Jessica has never been _____ Australia.

    c) What do you think _____ my new dress?

    d) The new boy in our class is _____ Singapore.

    e) I am waiting _____ you at the bus stop.

> to   in
> at
> for   of
> from
> on   after

20. Sally shows her friends pictures from her holidays.
    What is happening in the pictures?
    Example: Mike ___is eating___ fish. (eat)

    a) What are you _____ in this picture? (do)

    b) I _____ a large watermelon I bought at the market. (carry)

    c) The dress I _____ in this picture is new. (wear)

    d) The sun _____ in every picture. (shine)

    e) Here we _____ down to the beach. (go)

21. Put the verbs in the "going-to-form".

    a) I _____ (meet) Jane on Saturday for breakfast.

    b) On Monday I _____ (see) the doctor.

    c) I _____ (go) camping with some of my friends.

18 | Kompetenzbereich: Sprachgebrauch

22. Put the verbs in brackets into the simple past.

On Saturday morning Kelly and Sara _____ (meet) in town to do some shopping. They _____ (be) invited to a birthday party in the evening and _____ (want) to buy a present. At first they _____ (cannot) really decide what to buy, but then they _____ (see) a cool smartphone case and _____ (be) sure that that would be the right present for Tim. Now they _____ (can) take a look around for some trendy clothes for the party. Kelly _____ (buy) a T-shirt, but Sara _____ (does not) find anything. Afterwards they _____ (go) home to get changed for the party.

23. Fill in the correct tense.

   a) I _____ (feel) very sick yesterday, so I went to bed early and now I _____ (feel) much better.

   b) In 1982, my brother _____ (be) born.

   c) I _____ (move) to Australia next October. I can't stand the English weather any longer.

   d) My aunt _____ (give) me this book for my birthday last week.

24. In the ticket shop. Put the verbs in brackets into the correct tense.

   a) _____ (you/have) tickets for the Rihanna concert?

   b) No, I'm sorry. We _____ (sell) the last one yesterday.

   c) What a pity! But what about the open air festival which _____ (take place) in August?

   d) Yes, we _____ (still have) tickets for the festival.

25. Find the correct endings to each sentence.

1	They bought the blue cupboard	A	every morning.
2	He eats toast for breakfast	B	tomorrow.
3	He's washing the dishes	C	two years ago.
4	She will call her best friend	D	at the moment.

1	2	3	4

© Melica. Shutterstock

Kompetenzbereich: Sprachgebrauch | **19**

26. Write down the adverbs.

Example: correct → _____correctly_____

a) glad → _____

b) easy → _____

c) good → _____

d) close → _____

27. Adverbs of frequency (e.g. always) can be signal words for the simple present. Underline the adverbs of frequency and fill in the correct verb form.

Example: Jane <u>never</u> _____gets up_____ early in the morning. *(aufstehen)*

a) Mum always _____ me up in the morning. *(aufwecken)*

b) Sally often _____ hiking at the weekends. *(gehen)*

c) Every year, Mr Jones _____ his holidays in Ireland. *(verbringen)*

d) On Mondays, Jane _____ always late for school. *(sein)*
   The rest of the week she usually _____ on time.
   (ankommen)

e) Lisa never _____ her homework properly. *(machen)*

28. Describe the people and make comparisons.

Example: Julia's hair is _____longer_____ *(long)* than Ian's.

a) Jessica is _____ *(tall)*
   than Jenny.

b) Jim is _____ *(tall)*
   boy in our class.

c) Sara has _____ *(long)*
   hair.

d) Michelle's hair is _____ *(dark)*
   than Tina's.

© swissmacky. Shutterstock

e) Toby is _____ *(good)* at playing football _____ Mark.

f) But Lisa is the _____ *(good)* player!

Kompetenzbereich: Sprachgebrauch

29. Comparisons: Danny and Luisa are talking about their holidays. Fill in the missing words.

The weather in France was much _____ (bad) than last year. It was raining almost all the time. Our flat, however, was _____ (comfortable) than last year. I also like the French food. It's much _____ (good) than the food in England. In my opinion, France is the _____ _____ (beautiful) country in Europe.

© Max Topchii. Shutterstock

I went to Spain with a youth group. The weather in San Sebastian was almost as _____ (bad) in France, but it was _____ (exciting) to spend the holidays there than with my parents in Scotland. In my opinion, Spanish food is the _____ (good) in Europe. My holiday in Spain was great, and I met _____ (many) people _____ in all my holidays before!

© darrinhenry. 123rf.com

30. Fill in the correct pronouns.

Mrs Brown comes into the classroom, looks out of the window and asks her class in surprise, "Whose jacket is that lying outside?" John answers, "_____ is Lisa's." "Lisa, is that true? Is that _____ jacket?" Mrs Brown asks. "Go and get _____, please." Then Mrs Brown notices that Lisa is not in the classroom. "Where is _____ today?" "_____ think _____ is ill," says Maggie, who sounds as if she has been crying, "_____ didn't wait for _____ this morning like _____ usually does. _____ borrowed _____ jacket yesterday and _____ told me to look after _____. But this morning, Jack and Tim took the jacket and threw _____ around. _____ couldn't catch _____, and then _____ threw _____ out of the window." "Is that true, _____ two?" asks Mrs Brown, "Did _____ do that? Go and get the jacket immediately, give _____ back to Maggie and say sorry to _____. _____ will stay behind after school and clean up the classroom." Jack is very angry and says, "_____ wasn't _____!" _____ points at Tim: "_____ did it – _____ was all _____ fault!" Mrs Brown turns to the whole class and says, "All of _____ saw _____ take the jacket and throw _____ out of the window, and did any of _____ help Maggie? No, _____ didn't. _____ have decided that _____ will

Kompetenzbereich: Sprachgebrauch 21

all stay behind after school and clean up the classroom. Maggie, _____ go to Lisa's house straight after school, return the jacket to _____ and explain what _____ did at school today. And now, everyone, please show _____ _____ homework!"

31. Fill in the missing relative pronoun (who/which).

a) Doesn't the pullover _____ is lying on the floor belong to you?

b) The man _____ lives next door had an accident yesterday.

c) The book _____ you lent me last week was really exciting.

d) The woman _____ is sitting next to you is my mother.

e) The train _____ arrived late was very crowded.

32. Fill in the words needed for the following if-clauses.

Example: If I _*am*_ nice, I will get a big birthday present. *(be)*

a) If I take the train, I _____ late. *(be)*

b) If you don't take an umbrella with you, you _____ wet. *(get)*

c) If I move to America, I _____ my English. *(improve)*

d) I _____ *(not tell)* you even if you ask me a hundred times.

33. Which parts go together? Draw lines.

a)	I would like	this pair of jeans	the menu, please.
b)	Could you tell me	a loaf of bread,	one size bigger?
c)	I'd like	to have	the next bus station?
d)	Do you have	the way to	please.

34. Form sentences. Use all the words.

Example: summer / a / holidays / start / few / weeks / the / in
The summer holidays start in a few weeks.

a) visit / in California / aunt and uncle / is going to / his
Paul _____

b) summer / the / with / invited / to spend / him / them
They _____

c) that / jealous / her / make / brother / is / a trip / is going to
Zoe _____

d) promises / can / that / she / them / aunt / visit / soon / too
Zoe's _____

Kompetenzbereich: Sprachgebrauch

35. Here are some answers. Write down the questions.

    a) _____
    I live in Berlin.

    b) _____
    I'm seventeen years old.

    c) _____
    I'm here to improve my English.

    d) _____
    Yes, I like this town very much.

    e) _____
    No, I've never been here before.

36. Make the following phrases negative. Use the short forms.
    Example: Susan likes learning vocabulary.
                 Susan doesn't like learning vocabulary.

    a) The sun is shining outside.
    _____

    b) Mr Weaver enjoyed the film he watched yesterday.
    _____

    c) The Smiths have a new car.
    _____

    d) Sara has a dog.
    _____

    e) The weather forecast says it will rain tomorrow.
    _____

    f) The Millers are travelling around Europe.
    _____

37. Read Jason's message and complete each gap with a suitable word. There is an example at the beginning.

    Hi Brian,

    Yesterday I met my tutor, Mr Castiello, (0) **at** school.

    He (1) _____ me a lot of questions,

    for example (2) _____

    my family or what it was like at my old

    school. He already knew that Maths

    is my favourite (3) _____

    so I'm going to be in an honors class again. The good news:

    © Regien Paassen. Shutterstock

Kompetenzbereich: Sprachgebrauch | **23**

(4) _____ is a football team at the new school (5) _____ I can join right away. The next practice is already tomorrow afternoon. This is great! Let's see (6) _____ good this team is and what matches they have with other schools. Thinking about it, my new school could actually (7) _____ quite OK!

Take care,

Jason

> **Fehler finden und verbessern**
> Bei diesem Aufgabenformat wird dir ein Text vorgelegt, der mehrere Fehler enthält. Markiere die Fehler und schreibe das richtige Wort jeweils auf die Linie neben dem Text. Du brauchst also nur in denjenigen Zeilen nach einem Fehler suchen, zu denen es auf der rechten Seite auch eine Linie gibt.

38. Read Jason's diary entry. There are six mistakes in the text. Find these mistakes and write the correct words on the numbered lines. There is an example at the beginning.

Dear diary,	
Today was <u>me</u> first day at the new school. It	**0. my**
was OK. I was a bit nervous because I am join-	
ing a new class in the middle for the year. All	1. _____
of the other students already know each other	
and I am the new kid. But my new teacher,	
Mrs Stephenson, was really nice and he intro-	2. _____
duced me to the whole class. There is 22 stu-	3. _____
dents in the class, just about as much girls as	4. _____
boys. I sit next to Justin, who also live in my	5. _____
neighborhood. Let's see, maybe we were be	6. _____
friends.	

3 Kompetenzbereich: Leseverstehen

Es gibt viele verschiedene Arten von Lesetexten. In der Quali-Prüfung wird dir meist ein Sachtext vorgelegt. Zu diesem Text musst du verschiedene Aufgaben bearbeiten. Die Aufgabenstellungen, die am häufigsten im Unterricht, in Proben und im Quali vorkommen, findest du auf den folgenden Seiten. Zu manchen dieser Aufgabenstellungen gibt es zusätzlich auch Tipps zur Bearbeitung.

3.1 Strategien zum Kompetenzbereich „Leseverstehen"

Arbeitsschritt 1
Zunächst einmal ist es sinnvoll, den Text, inklusive Überschrift, zu überfliegen, um einen Eindruck zu bekommen, um was es gehen könnte.

Arbeitsschritt 2
Als Nächstes solltest du den Text **genau lesen**. Unbekannte Wörter kannst du **im Wörterbuch nachschlagen**. Achte aber darauf, dass du nicht zu viele Wörter nachschaust, denn das kostet wertvolle Zeit. Manche Wörter kannst du außerdem leicht aus dem **Sinnzusammenhang erschließen**.
Ganz entscheidend ist, dass du dir bei diesem Arbeitsschritt einen guten Überblick über den Inhalt des Textes verschaffst.

Arbeitsschritt 3
Nun solltest du die **Aufgabenstellungen genau lesen**, damit du weißt, unter welchen Aspekten du den Text bearbeiten sollst. Lies den Lesetext ein weiteres Mal. **Markiere** dabei gezielt wichtige **Schlüsselwörter bzw. Textpassagen**, um sie bei der Bearbeitung der Aufgaben schnell wieder zu finden.

Nun bist du für die Beantwortung der Aufgaben gut gerüstet!

TIPP

- Lies den Text gründlich durch. Schlage unbekannte Wörter im Wörterbuch nach. Verschaffe dir so einen Überblick über den genauen Inhalt des Textes.
- Lies die Aufgabenstellungen genau. Markiere beim nochmaligen Lesen des Textes wichtige Textaussagen im Hinblick auf die Aufgabenstellungen.

Kompetenzbereich: Leseverstehen | 25

3.2 Übungsaufgaben zum Kompetenzbereich „Leseverstehen"

Test 1: Treasure hunting at the Florida Keys

Read the text and do the following tasks.

❶ "Today's the day" is what Mel Fisher, one of the world's greatest treasure hunters, used to say every day, while he was searching for the famous ship-
5 wreck of the Spanish galleon *Nuestra Señora de Atocha*, which had sunk in a hurricane near the Florida Keys in 1622. For years, Mel Fisher and his crew had been searching the sea near Florida for
10 the *Atocha's* treasure with dedication, hoping every day that they would finally find the ship.

❷ Before they started with treasure hunting, Mel and his wife Dolores had
15 already had a lot of experience with diving: they had a "dive shop" in California and had given scuba diving trainings. In 1962, Mel started searching for shipwrecks off the East Coast of Florida
20 by diving. After almost one year of not finding anything, his crew finally found the first treasure: one thousand gold coins. Mel Fisher shouted: "If you once see the ocean bottom full of gold,
25 you'll never forget it!" Afterwards, he simply couldn't stop treasure hunting and it became his family business.

❸ In 1969, Mel began to search the sea around the Florida Keys for the
30 *Atocha*. This ship, with valuable goods from South America aboard, was part of a fleet of 28 ships on their way from Havanna, Cuba, to Spain. On 5th September, 1622, the *Atocha* sank in a
35 hurricane – 260 people drowned and only five were rescued. The ship would remain unfound at the bottom of the sea for the next 362 years.

The search was accompanied by a big
40 personal tragedy for Mel Fisher: In 1975, one of Mel's sons and his daughter-in-law were killed when their boat sank.

In 1980, Mel discovered gold and other
45 riches worth 20 million dollars in the wreck of the *Santa Margarita*, a sister ship of the *Atocha*, lost in the same hurricane of 1622.

❹ Then, on 20th July, 1985, it was
50 "the day" when Mel Fisher's dream finally came true and the fabulous treasure was found. After a search of 16 years, Mel's son Kane and his crew discovered the *Atocha* at a depth of only
55 16 metres below sea level. Crew members, who had dived to the bottom of the sea, were thrilled, and said the treasure looked like a "reef" of silver bars. The *Atocha's* cargo was indeed
60 one of the biggest treasures ever found. It was worth about 450 million dollars, and included 40 tons of gold and silver as well as emeralds and many artefacts. A team of archeologists was brought
65 together to make sure that the treasure and other parts from the ship were collected properly and did not get damaged.

❺ Today, Mel Fisher's Museum in Key
70 West, Florida, contains a great collection of artefacts from the *Atocha* and the *Santa Margarita*. Among the treasures are also a lot of objects that tell us about life in the seventeenth century:
75 navigational instruments, military equipment, objects of native American origin, tools, ceramics, even seeds and insects. Approximately 200,000 people visit the museum every year to see
80 these cultural and historical treasures.

❻ Although Mel Fisher died in 1998, the family business has continued until today because the family are convinced that there are still many treasures to be
85 found in shipwrecks. They even offer scuba diving tours for tourists to the site of the *Atocha* shipwreck. Having seen all the great treasures in the museum, the excited tourists follow Mel
90 Fisher's motto: "Today's the day!"

Kompetenzbereich: Reading

1. Match the correct titles (A–G) to each paragraph (❶–❻). Write the correct letters in the boxes. Use each letter only once. There is one extra title. One example is already given.

    A   A museum for the public
    B   Mel Fisher's submarine
    C̶   Mel Fisher and his motto
    D   The big treasure finally found
    E   The sinking of the *Atocha* and the hardships during the search
    F   Treasure hunting tours
    G   The beginnings of Mel Fisher's treasure hunting

paragraph ❶ (lines 1–12)	C
paragraph ❷ (lines 13–27)	
paragraph ❸ (lines 28–48)	
paragraph ❹ (lines 49–68)	
paragraph ❺ (lines 69–80)	
paragraph ❻ (lines 81–90)	

TIPP

> **True, false, not in the text**
> Hier wird dir eine Aussage vorgelegt und du musst entscheiden, ob sie richtig (T = *true*) ist oder falsch (F = *false*) oder ob dazu gar keine Informationen im Text vorhanden sind. Wenn du also eine Aussage im Text nicht findest, musst du „N" (= *not in the text*) ankreuzen. Beachte, dass die Aussagen manchmal etwas anders formuliert sind als der entsprechende Satz im Text.

2. Are the statements true (T), false (F) or not in the text (N)? Tick (✓) the correct box. An example is already given.

    Example: Mel Fisher is one of the world's best sailors. T ☐ F ✓ N ☐

    a) The *Atocha* was a Spanish ship.
    b) Mel Fisher and his wife Dolores had a surf shop in California.
    c) Mel and Dolores married in 1953.
    d) The *Atocha* was on her way to Havanna when she sank.
    e) The treasure is worth about 40 million dollars.
    f) You can also go on diving tours to the shipwreck site.

© Ocean Image Photography. Shutterstock

3. Match the correct dates and events. There is one extra sentence. One example is already given.

   ① 1622   A   Mel Fisher's son Kane is born
   ② 1962   B   Mel Fisher begins his search for treasure
   ③ 1969   C   *Atocha* shipwreck is found
   ④ 1975   D   Loss of family members in a boat accident
   ⑤ 1980   E   Mel Fisher passes away
   ⑥ 1985   F   Start of Mel's search for the *Atocha*
   ⑦ 1998   G $ 20 million treasure found
            H   The *Atocha* sinks

①	②	③	④	⑤	⑥	⑦
H						

4. Answer the questions using information from the text. Write short answers. There is an example at the beginning.

   Example: What happened to the *Atocha* in the year 1622?
   It sank in a hurricane.

   a) What did Mel Fisher do before he became a professional treasure hunter?
   _____

   b) How many people survived when the *Atocha* sank?
   _____

   c) What was the *Santa Margarita*?
   _____

   d) Why did archeologists help collect the treasures of the *Atocha*?
   _____

   e) What objects can you see in the Fisher Museum? (4 examples)
   _____
   _____
   _____
   _____

© Can Stock Photo/ IvonneWierink

Test 2: Camels in Australia

Read the text and do the following tasks.

1 On one day every year, there is a lot of excitement in the town of Alice Springs, Australia, when the annual Camel Cup takes place. Set under bright
5 blue skies in the dusty red scenery of the Outback, cameleers get together to race their camels and to have a lot of fun. Having started in 1970 because of a bet between two friends, Noel Fullerton
10 and Keith Mooney-Smith, the event has now been held for over forty years and attracts thousands of people. Even today, Noel Fullerton is still active in the Cup as he provides most of the
15 camels and as he is like a father figure. Another key person of the event is Neil Waters: he has been riding in the Cup since 1978 and has won many races. ❶

20 Did you know that Australia has the largest population of feral (wild) camels in the world? Of over 300,000 camels living in the desert regions of the Australian continent in 2013, most are so-
25 called dromedaries (the ones that have one hump). ❷ During the colonisation of Australia, people used camels as transport animals because they are used to a hot and dry climate. A bull camel
30 can carry up to 600 kg and camel treks can travel up to 40 km a day.

The first camels were imported by ship from India and Afghanistan in the 19th century. In 1846, the adventurer John
35 Horrocks was the first person to use a camel for an inland exploration. His camel had come to Australia in 1840, and was named Harry. Unfortunately, Horrocks was injured by camel Harry
40 while hunting and died because of his wounds. ❸

Later, many camel expeditions were done with the help of cameleers from the Arab world and by the end of the
45 19th century over 15,000 camels had been imported to Australia. ❹ Camels were, for example, used in the construction of the Overland Telegraph Line and of the water supply infrastruc-
50 ture in Western Australia.

In the early 20th century, motorised vehicles replaced camels as a means of transport. Many camels were simply set free into the wild. The feral camel
55 population has grown quickly since, and its great number causes problems for the environment: camels eat 80% of the plant species. The animals also pollute water holes in the desert and dam-
60 age man-made water systems. Therefore, in 2009, a programme to manage and control the size of the wild camel population in Australia was started with a budget of 19 million Australian
65 dollars. Over 160,000 camels have been killed since then. ❺ Today, camel meat from Australia is exported to other parts of the world like Europe, the US and Japan. ❻ There is an in-
70 dustry of camel milk products as well. Live camels are exported to the Arab world for the breeding of race camels.

© John Carnemolla. Shutterstock

Kompetenzbereich: Leseverstehen | 29

TIPP

Multiple choice
Hier bekommst du Fragen mit verschiedenen Antwortmöglichkeiten, oder du musst die richtigen Satzenden auswählen. Beachte dabei, dass diese häufig anders formuliert sind als im Text. Versuche, die richtige Antwort herauszufinden. Wenn du dir unsicher bist, dann suche zuerst die Antworten, die falsch sind. Die Reihenfolge der Fragen entspricht meist dem Textaufbau, sodass du abschätzen kannst, wo im Text die Antwort stehen muss.

1. Finish the sentences. Tick (✓) the correct box. You will find the answers in the text.

   a) The Camel Cup takes place in …
      - [ ] Austria.
      - [ ] Australia.
      - [ ] Alice Cooper.
      - [ ] Fullerton.

   b) The Camel Cup is a …
      - [ ] fun park.
      - [ ] zoo in the Outback.
      - [ ] camel race.
      - [ ] camel farm.

   © Kevin Autret. Shutterstock

   c) Noel Fullerton …
      - [ ] made a bet with a friend.
      - [ ] is not interested in the Cup any longer.
      - [ ] is 70 years old.
      - [ ] is married.

   d) Most wild camels in the world can be found in …
      - [ ] Africa.
      - [ ] India.
      - [ ] Afghanistan.
      - [ ] Australia.

   e) The first camels were imported to Australia because …
      - [ ] of the merchant's good prices.
      - [ ] they were used to find water in the desert.
      - [ ] they can transport goods and are used to the heat.
      - [ ] John Horrocks didn't want to do an exploration with a horse.

   f) To manage the wild camel population …
      - [ ] Australians built new water tanks.
      - [ ] 80 % of the plant species were polluted.
      - [ ] motorised vehicles were used in the 20th century.
      - [ ] Australians spend a lot of money.

Kompetenzbereich: Leseverstehen

2. Six sentences are missing in the text "Camels in Australia". Read the sentences A–G and match them with the gaps (①–⑥) in the text. There is one extra sentence. Gap ① is already matched.

   A The camel was shot.
   B The rabbit-proof fence stretches through Western Australia over a distance of 3,256 km.
   C Most of them were shot out of helicopters or out of vehicles on the ground.
   D There are also Bactrian camels (which have two humps).
   E Today he and his wife own the camel farm "Camels Australia", 90 km south of Alice Springs, which is also a tourist attraction.
   F For some years it was also used in the production of pet food.
   G The camel business was dominated by Muslim merchants.

①	②	③	④	⑤	⑥
E					

3. Which line or lines from the text tell(s) you that …

   Example: the Camel Cup takes place every year?   (lines) 1–4

   a) a lot of people are interested in the Cup?   _____
   b) male camels are very strong?   _____
   c) camels have not always lived in Australia?   _____
   d) the Arab world is interested in live Australian camels?   _____

4. Answer the questions using information from the text. Write short answers. There is one example at the beginning.

   Example: How many wild camels lived in Australia in 2013?
       over 300,000

   a) How far can camel treks travel per day?
   _____

   b) What happened to John Horrocks?
   _____

   c) Why have camels become a pest in Australia? (2 examples)
   _____
   _____

   d) Give two examples of camel business in Australia today.
   _____
   _____

Test 3: Is autonomous driving becoming a reality?

Read the text and do the following tasks.

A The state of California has been taking the lead in allowing self-driving cars – or "autonomous driving" – in traffic, but there are strict rules: for example, cars must still have a steering wheel, and there is still a driver with a driving licence, who sits behind the wheel to take control if the machine fails. Another important rule: it is still the driver of the vehicle – and not the manufacturer – who is made responsible in case of an accident.

B The highest priority of autonomous driving is the safety of persons, inside and outside the car. While the key intention of introducing autonomous driving is to increase traffic safety, there are also new risks. This is why the state of California also requests that measures are taken against computer hackers trying to manipulate car software. Just imagine hackers taking control of self-driving cars and steering them anywhere they like or even causing an accident!

C In modern cars there are already so-called "advanced driver assistance systems" (ADAS): They increase passenger safety and improve the driving of the car. The systems alert the driver of potential problems or avoid collisions. The car, for example, takes control of its speed, or it brakes automatically in case of danger. Intelligent car communication therefore helps the driver to avoid danger or problems: Traffic warnings from the radio allow one to plan which route to take. The car may also warn the drivers when they leave the correct lane, or it shows what is in the "blind spots".

D However, there is still a long way to go to the fully self-driving car, which, for example, won't have a steering wheel at all! Besides avoiding human errors and therefore increasing traffic safety, it is expected that autonomous driving will make traffic smoother and that more cars can use the roads, also at higher speeds. Age or physical ability of drivers would not matter anymore because driving would be automatic. Traffic signs would become unnecessary as cars would communicate electronically. The driver would simply become a passenger.

E Still, there will be more political debate about autonomous driving. First of all, there could still be critical traffic situations requiring human interaction. However, the passengers might not have enough experience in driving anymore. And what are the people going to do whose job was to drive a car or a truck? How about the loss of privacy if your car sends all sorts of information to other cars or the traffic system? And finally, who is to blame if an accident happens? Will the car manufacturers take the responsibility?

F California is taking the lead for setting up regulations for autonomous driving, which might become the model for the rest of the United States. A number of car manufacturers like Tesla, Ford and Toyota are developing autonomous cars. Other companies, which are originally no car manufacturers, such as Google, have also started developing autonomous driving systems. Toyota announced it would invest one billion dollars in the development of artificial intelligence (AI) for cars. Some experts are sceptical that AI is going to be available soon and they believe that fully self-driving cars are still science fiction. However, experts of the Institute of Electrical and Electronics Engineers (IEEE) estimate that by the year 2040 75 % of all cars will be driving autonomously.

1. Find the correct titles (1–8) for the paragraphs. There are three extra titles. Use each number only once. One title is already matched (0).

    ⓪ First steps towards autonomous driving
    ① Political issues regarding autonomous driving
    ② Pollution caused by self-driving cars
    ③ Car manufacturers and IT companies develop AI for cars
    ④ Advanced driver assistance systems already available
    ⑤ Driving schools are concerned about their future
    ⑥ Benefits of autonomous driving
    ⑦ Safety comes first
    ⑧ European governments promote autonomous driving

paragraph A	paragraph B	paragraph C	paragraph D	paragraph E	paragraph F
0					

2. Five of the statements are true. Select the true statements according to the information in the text. Note the letters of the true statements on the lines next to the box. An example is already given (0).

    a **California has been first to allow self-driving cars in the streets.**
    b The rules for autonomous driving are strict.
    c The US government spends about $ 1 billion to sue computer hackers of car systems.
    d Advanced driver assistance programmes help drivers to avoid accidents.
    e Self-driving cars have many advantages.
    f There's no difference between cars with advanced driver assistance programmes and fully self-driving cars.
    g Once all cars are electronically controlled, traffic signs won't be needed any more.
    h Autonomous driving has no risks.
    i California plays an important role in creating traffic signs.
    j It is estimated that more than half of all cars will be self-driving by 2040.

    True statements:
    0. a
    1. _____
    2. _____
    3. _____
    4. _____
    5. _____

13. Which line(s) from the text tell you the same as the following expressions? Write the number of the line(s) in the box below. There is an example at the beginning (0).

    0. Automated cars still have a driver who can take control when necessary.
    1. Something has to be done against people who illegally try to change the software programme of a car.
    2. Drivers may be alerted by the car system in case they use the wrong lane.
    3. When "driving" an automated car it is not important how old or physically fit you are.
    4. People with jobs related to transport might lose their jobs.
    5. Even companies that did business outside the automobile industry so far are entering the market of self-driving cars.

0	1	2	3	4	5
line(s) 5–9	line(s)	line(s)	line(s)	line(s)	line(s)

14. The following words have different meanings. Which of the meanings below is the one used in the text? Tick (✓) the correct meaning. An example is already given.

    a) state (line 1)
       ☐ Zustand (Nomen)
       ☐ Rang (Nomen)
       ✓ Staat (Nomen)
       ☐ nennen (Verb + Objekt)

    b) case (line 12)
       ☐ Koffer (Nomen)
       ☐ Fall (Nomen)
       ☐ Schachtel (Nomen)
       ☐ inspizieren (Verb + Objekt)

    c) key (line 15)
       ☐ wichtigste/wesentliche (Adjektiv)
       ☐ Taste (Nomen)
       ☐ etw. auf etw./jmd. abstimmen (Verb + Objekt)
       ☐ etw. eingeben (Verb + Objekt)

    d) alert (line 30)
       ☐ aufmerksam (Adjektiv)
       ☐ warnen (Verb + Objekt)
       ☐ Alarm (Nomen)
       ☐ wachsam (Adjektiv)

    e) lead (line 71)
       ☐ Kabel (Nomen)
       ☐ Führung (Nomen)
       ☐ Leine (Nomen)
       ☐ führen (Verb + Objekt)

© Foto: Walter Shick, CC BY-SA 4.0

Test 4: Kelechi Iheanacho

Read the text and do the following tasks.

1 Kelechi Promise Iheanacho lives the dream of millions of young Africans who want to become world-class football stars. 'Kel', as his friends call him,
5 was born in Nigeria on 3rd October, 1996. Just over twenty years later, he has become a member of the Nigerian national football team. From 2015 to 2017 he played for the top Premier
10 League team Manchester City and now plays for Leicester City. Kelechi's inspiring story is that of a young man who wants to contribute
15 by doing his very best.
In an interview Kelechi says that his success of joining the "first team" of Manchester City is
20 due to his hard work with the club's U-21 development squad, while he still dreams of going higher. Being in the
25 team of the best, however, brings with it a lot of pressure and a high level of expectation. It was his dream to be in
30 the first team, but when he was finally called to join, it still came as a surprise to him.
Kelechi's football career started while he was playing in the U-17 for Imo
35 state, Nigeria, and several European clubs were closely following his performance in the 2013 FIFA U-17 World Cup. In the interview, Kelechi says that he thought he was too small to go to
40 the U-17 and that when he saw the big boys playing he didn't know if he could make it. However, due to his coach's support and his great performance, he did. In the same year, he also
45 received the title of "Most Promising Talent of the Year" from the Confederation of African Football. On his 18th birthday Kelechi joined Manchester City.
50 As his middle name "Promise" suggests, Kelechi is a model for many young Africans who aspire to a successful career in football. He explains that life in Africa can be hard. But with
55 devotion, he overcame all obstacles: Although his parents at first did not want him to play football and told him to stop playing and go to school instead, he was
60 stubborn. And even if he didn't have a ball, he would play with stones while he was walking in the road.
65 Kelechi's father was a trader and his mother a teacher, who unfortunately died a few years ago. This was a really
70 hard experience for the young football star and his family. As he still has two brothers and a sister back in Nigeria, Kelechi
75 makes a special effort for his deceased mother and his family, which gives him strength – also because he lives on his own. At first, Ke-
80 lechi was impressed by Manchester City's big team and fantastic players, so he did not think that he would have a future there. However, his father supported him and gave him confidence.
85 Kelechi thinks that a lot of kids in his home country are inspired by his story and by what he achieved at quite a young age.
Kelechi Iheanacho is focused on giving
90 his very best for Leicester City, too, while following his dream to become a great player. He wants to contribute to the team's success and to work hard every day.

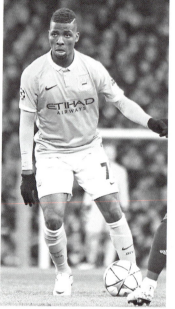

Foto: © Julicos/Dreamstime.com-Kelechi Iheanacho Photo

Kompetenzbereich: Leseverstehen | 35

11. Are the statements true (T), false (F) or not in the text (N) according to the information given in the text? Tick (✓) the correct box.
An example is already given.

		T	F	N
Example:	Kelechi has always worked very hard to make his dream come true.	✓	☐	☐
a)	Kelechi plays for the national football team of Nigeria and played for the first team of Manchester City.	☐	☐	☐
b)	Kelechi never had any doubts that he would make it to the top.	☐	☐	☐
c)	Besides a Nigerian passport, Kelechi also has a British passport.	☐	☐	☐
d)	Kelechi still has family in Nigeria.	☐	☐	☐
e)	It was Kelechi's dream to become team captain of Manchester City one day.	☐	☐	☐
f)	Kelechi lives together with his father.	☐	☐	☐

12. Put the following facts into the correct chronological order.
One statement is wrong. There is an example at the beginning.

a	**Kelechi Promise Iheanacho is born.**
b	Kelechi changes to FC Liverpool.
c	Kelechi plays in Manchester City's first team.
d	Kelechi plays for the U-17 in Nigeria.
e	As a boy he prefers playing football to attending school.
f	Kelechi joins Manchester City in the U-21 development squad.

True statements:

0. a

1. _____

2. _____

3. _____

4. _____

Answering questions

Manchmal musst du auch Fragen in kurzen Sätzen oder in Stichworten beantworten. Lies dir die Fragen genau durch. Finde Stichwörter oder auch Zahlen (z. B. „2013", „dream"), die in der Frage erwähnt werden, und suche sie im Text, sodass du die Stelle findest, die dir die richtige Antwort auf die gestellte Frage gibt.

---

13. Answer the questions using information from the text.
Write short answers. There is an example at the beginning.

Example: When is Kelechi's birthday?

3rd October 1996

a) In which country did Kelechi's career as a footballer start?

_____

36 | **Kompetenzbereich: Leseverstehen**

b) Which award did Kelechi receive in 2013?

_____

c) How old was Kelechi when he joined Manchester City?

_____

d) How many brothers and sisters does Kelechi
have in Nigeria?

_____

_____

e) What is Kelechi's dream?

_____

_____

© Le Do.
Shutterstock

4. Which part from the text gives you the following information?
Write down the number of the line or lines.
An example is already given.

Example:
Manchester City is one of the best English clubs.   (lines) 9/10

a) Kelechi did not expect to make it into the first
team of Manchester City.   _____

b) Kelechi is a good example to lots of his countrymen.   _____

c) Kelechi's mum passed away.   _____

d) Kelechi's father believes in him.   _____

e) He tries to support his team to win.   _____

4 Kompetenzbereich: Sprachmittlung

Der Bereich „Sprachmittlung" kommt mit der Quali-Prüfung 2022 neu hinzu. Dabei handelt es sich um das sinngemäße Übertragen von der einen in die andere Sprache. Im Quali wirst du durch die Aufgabenstellung in eine bestimmte Situation versetzt, in der du englische Inhalte auf Deutsch wiedergeben sollst.

Die Grundlage für die Sprachmittlung im Quali bilden englische Texte. Häufig sind dies Informationstexte, z. B. aus einem Reiseführer oder einem Flyer. Mit Hilfe der Informationen, die im Ausgangstext enthalten sind, sollen dann die zugehörigen Aufgaben bearbeitet werden. Basierend auf dem Ausgangstext musst du z. B. auf Deutsch einen Beitrag für die Schülerzeitung schreiben, eine E-Mail verfassen oder einen Steckbrief bzw. einen Chatverlauf ergänzen.

4.1 Strategien zum Kompetenzbereich „Sprachmittlung"

Lies zunächst die Aufgabenstellung durch, damit du weißt, um was es geht und was du machen sollst.

Arbeitsschritt 1

Lies den englischen Text durch und verschaffe dir einen Überblick über den Inhalt. Unbekannte Wörter solltest du nur nachschlagen, wenn du sie nicht aus dem Zusammenhang erschließen kannst und du wichtige Zusammenhänge sonst nicht verstehst.

Arbeitsschritt 2

Gehe die Aufgabenstellung erneut durch. Markiere im englischen Text alle Inhalte, die du zur Bearbeitung der Aufgabe benötigst. Überlege nun, wie du diese Textstellen auf Deutsch wiedergeben könntest. Es wird nicht erwartet, dass du alles 1:1 übersetzt, sondern dass du den Sinn erfasst und in deinen eigenen Worten zum Ausdruck bringst.

Arbeitsschritt 3

Bearbeite nun die Aufgabe auf Deutsch. Beachte dabei alle Vorgaben: Welches Textformat ist gefordert und was musst du daher beachten? Sollst du einen Lückentext ergänzen, einen persönlichen Brief oder einen sachlichen Artikel schreiben? Musst du in Stichpunkten antworten oder einen zusammenhängenden Text schreiben? Hast du die Vorgaben zum Umfang beachtet?

Arbeitsschritt 4

TIPP

- Verschaffe dir einen Überblick über den Inhalt des englischen Textes.
- Versuche zu verstehen, was in der Aufgabe genau verlangt wird.
- Markiere diejenigen Informationen im englischen Text, die du für die Aufgabe benötigst.
- Bearbeite die Aufgabe auf Deutsch. Berücksichtige alle geforderten Informationen und beachte das geforderte Format (z. B. E-Mail).

Die nachfolgenden Übungen bereiten dich auf die Aufgaben im Quali vor. Der Schwierigkeitsgrad der Übungen steigt dabei zunehmend.

4.2 Übungsaufgaben zum Kompetenzbereich „Sprachmittlung"

Test 1: Signs and posters

1. Du machst mit deiner Familie eine Rundreise in den USA. Dein kleiner Bruder versteht noch kein Englisch, also erklärst du ihm, was auf den folgenden Schildern steht.

a)

b)

c)

d)

e)

Abb. von oben nach unten: © FloridaStock. Shutterstock, © northallertonman. Shutterstock, © Sundry Photography. Shutterstock, © Jojoo64. Shutterstock, © Thomas Bullock. 123rf.com

Kompetenzbereich: Sprachmittlung 39

2. Dein kleiner Bruder sieht am 14. Oktober folgendes Plakat und möchte wissen, was darauf steht. Beantworte seine Fragen auf Deutsch.

© Vector Tradition SM. Fotolia.com

a) Auf dem Plakat steht etwas von einem „Festival", oder? Was ist es denn für eines?

_____
_____
_____

b) Wann findet es statt? Vielleicht können wir hingehen.

_____
_____

c) Das würde ja klappen. Was gibt es denn dort?

_____
_____
_____

d) Klingt gut. Muss man denn Eintritt zahlen?

_____
_____

3. Du bist mit deinen Großeltern im Urlaub. Deine Oma möchte wissen, was auf der folgenden Tafel steht, da sie kaum Englisch versteht. Beantworte ihre Fragen auf Deutsch.

© Can Stock Photo/kevers

Worterklärung: *bap* = eine Art Brötchen

a) „Breakfast" heißt doch „Frühstück", oder? Was wird denn angeboten und wieviel kostet es jeweils?

_____
_____
_____
_____

Kompetenzbereich: Sprachmittlung 41

b) Das ist alles? Gibt es noch mehr?

c) Sind wir noch rechtzeitig dran? Bis wann gibt es denn Frühstück?

d) Heute ist so ein schöner Tag. Vielleicht können wir das Frühstück auch mitnehmen und im Park essen. Geht das?

Test 2: Wimbledon

Für den Sportunterricht soll deine Gruppe ein Portfolio über das Thema „Tennis" erstellen. Du musst dabei eine Übersichtsseite zu Wimbledon verfassen. Verwende das folgende Faktenwissen zu dem berühmten Tennisturnier, um die Bilder auf der nächsten Seite in ganzen Sätzen auf Deutsch zu beschriften.

© Alex Staroseltsev. Shutterstock

> The Wimbledon Championships are the most famous tennis tournament in the world and have been held at Wimbledon, London, since 1877. They are the only Grand Slam event played on grass courts.

> Traditional dress code: there is no special dress code for visitors, but all tennis players must wear white or at least "almost entirely white" clothing.

> The Championships were cancelled in 2020 – for the first time since World War II – because of the COVID-19 pandemic.

> The term "Centre Court" comes from the arrangement of the tennis courts at Wimbledon, where the most important court is traditionally located in the middle of all the other courts. Today's Centre Court at Wimbledon seats 15,000 people.

> The Royal Box, at the south end of Centre Court, is reserved for the Royal Family or other VIPs. Today, players are obliged to bow (men) or curtsy (women) if the Queen or the Prince of Wales are there.

> Fans without tickets can watch the matches at Aorangi Terrace, a grassed area outside, on a giant television screen.

> BBGs – ball boys and ball girls – are important helpers at the tournament. They are 15 years old on average and come from local schools.

> Strawberries and cream are the traditional dessert at Wimbledon. Quantities consumed every year: 2 million strawberries and 7,000 litres of cream.

> There are different ways to get a ticket for Wimbledon:
> Apply and participate in a kind of lottery or queue overnight for a match on the following day – which is considered a typical part of the Wimbledon experience.

> The trophies are
> - a silver cup with a layer of gold (Men's Singles matches)
> - a silver salver called "Venus Rosewater Dish" (Ladies' Singles matches)

> Prize money in 2019:
> Winners of the Gentlemen's or Ladies' single matches: £ 2,350,000
> Winners of the Gentlemen's or Ladies' double matches (per pair): £ 540,000

Faktenwissen Wimbledon:

Beispiel:

In Wimbledon kann man folgende Trophäen gewinnen: den silbernen „Venus Rosewater"-Teller im Einzelfinale der Damen und einen silber-goldenen Pokal im Einzelfinale der Herren.

Abb. von oben nach unten: © Benjamí Villoslada i Gil/Wikipedia, CC BY-SA 2.0, © elvob/Wikipedia, CC BY-SA 2.0, CC BY-SA 4.0, © Can Stock Photo/Stocksolutions, © CC BY-SA 4.0, © GATORFAN2525/Wikipedia, © CC BY-SA 4.0

Test 3: Bungee jumping rules

Deine Tante hat vor, einen Bungee-Sprung zu machen. Da du dich für ein Englischprojekt gerade intensiv mit diesem Thema beschäftigst, kannst du ihr einiges darüber erzählen.
Lies zunächst den folgenden Text und bearbeite anschließend die Aufgabe.

Bungee jumping in New Zealand

Your bungee jump in New Zealand should be as memorable as possible. So keep these instructions in mind for a safe and unforgettable experience:

- Wear hiking boots as well as thick clothing to protect yourself from injury.
- Wearing a helmet is mandatory to protect your head!
- Feel positive! Having negative feelings could distract you from the jump, which is a risk.
- Do not jump in case of illnesses such as heart problems, high blood pressure, back problems, or if you are pregnant.
- Do not wear glasses as these could distract you, or they could break or get lost.
- Empty all pockets before jumping (e.g. smartphones) and make sure that your clothing is not too loose or too tight.
- Do not drink alcohol.
- Always follow the instructions of the crew.

Your Jump: Procedure

- You will receive thorough instructions on how to jump and react during your jump.
- Before entering the platform, two members of our staff help you put on a harness and double check to make sure everything is secure.
- If you are really cool, try not to scream as you jump, but of course it's OK if you do.
- After the jump you will be released from the cord and staff on the river will pick you up with a small boat and bring you ashore.

Abb. Hintergrund © Can Stock Photo/fosin2

Kompetenzbereich: Sprachmittlung | 45

Fasse die wichtigsten Informationen für deine Tante auf Deutsch zusammen.
Gehe dabei auf folgende Punkte ein:

1. Ausrüstung
2. Verbote
3. Vorgehen nach dem Sprung
4. Zwei weitere Tipps für deine Tante (die du bei 1. bis 3. noch nicht erwähnt hast)

Liebe Tante Emina,

du überlegst doch schon seit einiger Zeit, einmal einen Bungee-Sprung zu machen.
Ich habe darüber ein paar interessante Informationen gefunden:

Hoffentlich hilft dir das, eine Entscheidung zu treffen.

Viele Grüße,
(dein Name)

Senden

Test 4: Undara Lava Tubes

Du verbringst mit deinen Eltern die Sommerferien in Queensland, Australien. Während ihr einen ruhigen Tag am Strand der Stadt Cairns verbringt, suchst du im Internet nach Ausflugszielen. Dabei stößt du auf Informationen über die *Undara Lava Tubes*, die im Landesinneren von Queensland liegen. Lies zunächst den folgenden Text und bearbeite anschließend die Aufgabe.

The Undara Lava Tubes are located in northern Queensland, 275 km southwest of the coastal city of Cairns. They are an extensive region of underground caves that were created by lava from the Undara volcano about 190,000 years ago. Circa 1550 km² of the surrounding region were affected by this volcanic activity.

Undara is the Aboriginal word for "a long way". The Australian natives were the only inhabitants of the land around Undara until the Europeans arrived and started to raise cattle there in the 1860s. By the 1890s, the lava tubes were already well known. Tourists have been able to visit them on guided tours since 1989. The Undara Volcanic National Park was established in 2009 in order to protect these impressive geological formations as well as the flora and fauna of the region. In the same year, the park was also declared as one of Queensland's "Q150 icons".

When visiting the Undara Lava Tubes, it is important to pay attention to the climate. From October to March it is the monsoon period, with hot and humid weather. The drier months from April to August are therefore more suitable for a visit. You should also not explore the park on your own as it can be dangerous. Hikers can fall into one of the many hidden holes in the ground where lava caves have collapsed. Some of the tubes also contain high concentrations of carbon dioxide, which brings with it the risk of suffocation. Fortunately, there are guided tours being offered at Undara. These inform visitors about how the land was formed by natural forces and climate change over hundreds of millions of years.

Due to its distance from the coast, a visit to Undara is best combined with an overnight stay. Exclusive accommodation is offered directly at the Undara Lava tubes: It is possible to sleep in one of several nicely restored railway carriages that are over 100 years old. The town of Mount Surprise is not too far away (58 km) – with only around 170 inhabitants, this Outback town is really small, but it offers a pub and a café, service stations, a caravan park and a motel.

Abb. von oben nach unten © Jane Farquhar, © JulieMay54 / Wikipedia, CC BY-SA 4.0

Kompetenzbereich: Sprachmittlung 47

1. Die *Undara Lava Tubes* haben dein Interesse geweckt. Du unterhältst dich mit deinem Vater über diese Ausflugsmöglichkeit. Ergänze das folgende Gespräch auf Deutsch mit Informationen aus dem Text.

Du:

Ich habe im Internet ein interessantes Ausflugsziel gefunden. Die „Undara Lava Tubes" im Undara-Vulkan-Nationalpark.

Wie ein Höhlensystem.

Dein Vater:

Wie kann ich mir die Lava-Tunnel vorstellen?

Wie weit sind die „Lava Tubes" von Cairns entfernt?

Wann sind sie denn entstanden?

„Undara" – hat dieser Name eigentlich eine besondere Bedeutung?

Seit wann können die Lava-Höhlen von Touristen besichtigt werden?

Ist es eine gute Idee, jetzt im August dort hinzufahren?

Ich überlege gerade, ob wir eine geführte Tour buchen sollten. Mit welchen Gefahren müssen wir rechnen, wenn wir die Lava-Tunnel allein erkunden?

Welche Übernachtungsmöglichkeiten gibt es in der Nähe der Lavahöhlen?

- Motel in Mount Surprise
-
-

Kompetenzbereich: Sprachmittlung

2. Deine Familie hat beschlossen, die *Undara Lava Tubes* zu besichtigen. Deshalb informierst du dich nun genau über das Tour-Angebot. Lies zunächst den folgenden Text und bearbeite anschließend die Aufgabe.

Visitor Information for Undara's Lava Tubes

Allow two hours to complete – runs mid-March till October – bookings essential.

An excellent concentrated visit to the lava tubes, plus other interesting environmental, geological and historical features pointed out and explained by your guide throughout the trip to and from the tubes. Visits up to three sections of lava tubes. Easy fitness level with boardwalks and steps.

Please call our reservations team to book.

Rates and Information

Adult Rate	$ 60.50
Child Rate	$ 32.00
Family Rate (2 adults and up to 4 children)	$ 185.00

Departs 8 am, 10:30 am and 1 pm. Bookings essential – all tours are subject to availability and weather conditions.

Please note this tour is not suitable for prams, wheelchairs, walking frames or guests with mobility concerns.

The Ultimate Introduction To Undara's Lava Tubes, https://www.undara.com.au/touring/archway-explorer

Erkläre deinen Eltern, was du über die Tour herausgefunden hast. Fasse die Informationen zusammen, indem du die folgenden Fragen in ganzen Sätzen beantwortest.

a) Zu welchen Uhrzeiten findet eine geführte Tour statt und wie lange dauert sie?

b) Was erwartet die Besucher*innen bei dieser Tour (2 Aspekte)?

c) Welche Anforderungen bzw. Einschränkungen sind zu beachten (2 Aspekte)?

Also, ich habe Folgendes herausgefunden …

5 Kompetenzbereich: Text- und Medienkompetenzen

Mit dem Kompetenzbereich „Text- und Medienkompetenzen" kommt ab dem Quali 2022 ein weiterer Prüfungsteil hinzu. Als Ausgangsmaterial wird dir hier ein englischsprachiger Text vorgelegt. Es kann sich dabei um die verschiedensten Textsorten handeln, so z. B. um eine Bastelanleitung, einen Tagebucheintrag, einen Chat, einen Informationstext oder auch eine Mischung daraus. Deine Aufgabe ist es nun, diesem Ausgangstext Informationen zu entnehmen, um damit auf Englisch z. B. ein Poster oder ein Formular zu vervollständigen oder eine E-Mail zu schreiben.

5.1 Strategien zum Kompetenzbereich „Text- und Medien- kompetenzen"

Lies zunächst die Aufgabenstellung durch, damit du weißt, worum es geht und was du tun sollst.

Arbeitsschritt 1

Verschaffe dir einen Überblick über den Inhalt des englischen Ausgangstextes einschließlich der Überschrift, wenn vorhanden. Schlage Wörter, die du unbedingt zum Verständnis brauchst, im Wörterbuch nach.

Arbeitsschritt 2

Lies die Aufgabenstellung noch einmal genau durch und markiere im Ausgangstext alle Informationen, die du für deine Schreibaufgabe benötigst. Manche Informationen kannst du dabei vielleicht auch schon z. B. am Rand zusammenfassen. Nun kannst du den englischen Text schreiben. Wichtig ist dabei, dass du erkennst, welche Art von Text gefordert ist, z. B eine Postkarte, ein Steckbrief oder eine Anleitung. Überlege, auf was du beim Verfassen deines Textes achten musst. Soll er vielleicht an eine bestimmte Person adressiert sein? Musst du eventuell eine bestimmte Anrede- und Schlussformel oder eine besonders höfliche Sprache verwenden?

Arbeitsschritt 3

Verfasse nun deinen Text auf Englisch. Du darfst beim Formulieren auf den Ausgangstext zurückgreifen und auch bestimmte Textbausteine übernehmen. Meistens wirst du diese aber vom Satzbau oder vom Inhalt her so anpassen bzw. ergänzen müssen, dass sie zu deinem Text passen.

Arbeitsschritt 4

TIPP

- Verschaffe dir einen Überblick über den Inhalt des Ausgangstextes.
- Erkenne, was in der Aufgabe gefordert ist und wie du sie gestalten sollst.
- Markiere diejenigen Informationen im Ausgangstext, die du für die Lösung der Aufgabe benötigst.
- Bearbeite die Aufgabe auf Englisch. Berücksichtige alle geforderten Informationen und beachte das Textformat (z. B. Steckbrief, Poster, E-Mail)

Die nachfolgenden Übungen bereiten dich auf die Aufgaben im Quali vor. Der Schwierigkeitsgrad der Übungen steigt dabei zunehmend.

5.2 Übungsaufgaben zum Kompetenzbereich „Text- und Medienkompetenzen"

Test 1: Bungee jumping in New Zealand

Read the following text about bungee jumping in New Zealand.
Then do the task.

To some travellers, a trip to New Zealand would not be complete without the experience of a bungy jump. This activity involves a person jumping from a great height, like from a bridge, a tower or a platform on a crane, while being safely connected to a cord. In New Zealand, there are many locations for bungee jumping and numerous providers offer bookings for this exciting activity. Jumping heights vary from several dozen metres to over a hundred metres, like from a 43-metre-high bridge over the Kawarau River – which was also the first commercial bungee jumping site in New Zealand – or the Nevis bungee jumping platform (134 metres above a canyon). Both locations are near Queenstown on the South Island.

The classical type of jump is from a bridge above a canyon towards the river below. Jumpers can choose whether they want to touch the surface of the water or stay dry.

Bungee jumping was first introduced commercially by the New Zealander AJ Hackett, who performed his first jump from Greenhithe Bridge in Auckland, New Zealand's capital, and went on to perform numerous jumps at different places in the country and abroad. This led to an increased public interest in the sport. Since the 1980s, several million successful jumps have taken place and safety standards have been established. However, despite all precautions, some people have died – mainly because the cord was too long. In other cases, participants became detached from the cord when using only an ankle attachment. Therefore commercial operators today also use body harnesses to secure the jumpers.

Kawarau Bridge near Queenstown
© Nicram Sabod. Shutterstock

You have to create a poster in English about "Bungee Jumping in New Zealand" for school. Fill in the missing parts of the poster with information from the text.

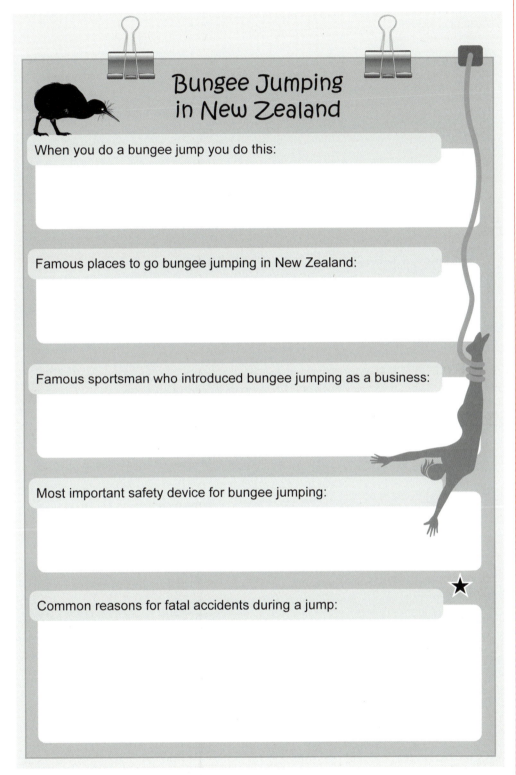

Clipboard © RaZZeRs. Shutterstock

52 | Kompetenzbereich: Text- und Medienkompetenzen

Test 2: Puppies

Janet is a student and gets a text message from her uncle Mike. Read the conversation between Janet and Mike. Then do the task.

It's so nice to hear from you again, Uncle Mike!
How are you doing and how is Mindy?
3:12 pm

I'm doing great! Guess what, I'm texting you because of Mindy.
3:13 pm ✓

Why? What happened?
3:13 pm

Gosh, you won't believe this: Mindy gave birth to some puppies six weeks ago.
3:15 pm ✓

Really? But that's wonderful! How many puppies are there?
3:17 pm

There are five: two female and three male ones.
3:18 pm ✓

Wow, five puppies. So you have six dogs in the house now?
3:19 pm

Right. But you know, that's also sort of the problem. I can't keep that many dogs and I'd like to give three puppies away.
3:21 pm ✓

Really?
3:21 pm

Yeah, I wanted to ask you if you'd like to have one of them ... or two?
3:23 pm ✓

Thanks for asking, that's so kind of you, and I'd like to have a puppy so much, but you know Mom doesn't let me keep any pets because of her allergies.
3:27 pm

Oh, sorry, I forgot about her allergies. I understand!
3:29 pm ✓

But I could put a post of your offer on our school website to say that you're giving some puppies away.
3:32 pm

Actually, that would be a good idea! Do you think any of your classmates would like to have a dog?
3:35 pm ✓

I'm pretty sure some of them would. OK, I'm going to write a post. Could you tell me some more things about the puppies – like what they look like or what breed they are?
3:40 pm

Well, they're mongrels. Mindy is a mixture between a terrier and a poodle. And I don't have any idea what the male dog was.
3:43 pm ✓

Kompetenzbereich: Text- und Medienkompetenzen | 53

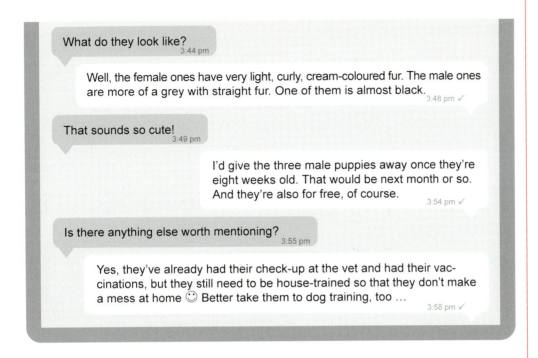

Help Janet to complete her post on the school website with information from the conversation.

Test 3: Postcard from Kovalam

Deepa is a schoolgirl from Bangalore, India, who is spending a weekend in the coastal town of Kovalam in the state of Kerala. Her aunt Divya and uncle Kumar live and work there as managers of a small hotel.
First, read the impressions Deepa wrote down in her diary:

"I like my aunt and uncle's hotel. True, it's a lot smaller and more old-fashioned than the big hotels on the seafront, but it's also less busy and the atmosphere is calm and relaxing. I have a small room to myself, but I hardly spend any time in it. There are so many things to see here so I'm outside all day while my relatives are busy working.

It is only a five-minute walk to the beach, where it's really quiet early in the morning. One morning, I sat down on the beach and a lady came by offering fresh fruit for sale, which she was carrying in a basket. Then I watched the fishermen bring in the nets, which took quite a long time. They looked disappointed as they hadn't caught a lot. After sitting in the sun for a while I went for a refreshing swim in the sea, wearing my dress like most Indian women do – not like the western tourists, who change into their bathing suits. I just love the sea, the warm water and the sandy beach! Back at the hotel I changed for lunch. Aunt Divya had already prepared one of her wonderful biryani meals – the way she cooks it is great: it's tasty and not too spicy.

In the afternoon, the seafront was already full of people. There were a lot of families, children and young couples going for a walk. There were also a lot of tourists from all over the world. The cafés and restaurants were crowded and everybody was having fun.
Well, it got too crowded for me, so I walked up to the Vizhinjam lighthouse and got a nice view of the coastline from the top. It's really nice here and I want to come again for sure. I think I should write a postcard to Mum and Dad …"

Abb. von oben nach unten © JMBryant/Wikipedia, mehul.antani/Wikipedia, CC BY 2.0

Now help Deepa write a postcard to her parents. Use relevant information from the text and write about:
- Deepa's accommodation
- beach life
- Deepa's activities
- sights

6 Kompetenzbereich: Schreiben

Viele Schülerinnen und Schüler sind der Meinung, dass sie sich auf den Bereich „Schreiben" nicht vorbereiten können, weil viel von der individuellen Einschätzung der Lehrkraft abhängt. Erschwerend kommen im Fach Englisch noch die Fremdsprache und die damit verbundenen Fehler hinzu. Aus diesen Gründen beschäftigen sich die meisten gar nicht erst mit diesem Kompetenzbereich. Das ist unklug, denn in diesem Teil kannst du die meisten Punkte erreichen. Mache nicht den gleichen Fehler und lies die folgenden Seiten gut durch. Du wirst sehen: Eine sinnvolle und erfolgreiche Vorbereitung auf das Verfassen englischer Texte ist möglich.

6.1 Strategien zum Kompetenzbereich „Schreiben"

Langfristige Vorbereitung

Genau wie auf den „Use of English"-Teil kannst du dich auf die Textproduktion in Proben und im Quali nur langfristig gut vorbereiten. Schaue dir z. B. englischsprachige Interviews mit deinen Lieblingsstars im Internet an, und lies viel auf Englisch. Besonders anfangs ist es empfehlenswert, eine Serie, die du schon kennst, oder einen Film, den du schon einmal in deiner Muttersprache gesehen hast, noch einmal auf Englisch (wahlweise auch mit Untertiteln) anzuschauen. Diese Sprachauswahl ist bei Streamingdiensten oder Blue Rays meist möglich. Du wirst sehen: Mit der Zeit verstehst du immer mehr und häufige Redewendungen werden dir vertraut.

Zu Übungszwecken kannst du auch digitale Wörterbücher nutzen. Gute Webseiten geben neben der einfachen Übersetzung auch Hinweise sowie Beispielsätze, um deutlich zu machen, in welchem Zusammenhang ein Wort verwendet werden kann.

Das Verfassen eines Textes

In der Prüfung hast du die Wahl zwischen den Aufgabentypen „**Creative Writing**" und „**Correspondence**". In der *Creative Writing*-Aufgabe wird dir ein Bild oder eine Bilderfolge vorgelegt, zu dem bzw. zu der du eine Geschichte verfassen sollst. Bei der *Correspondence*-Aufgabe schreibst du zu einem bestimmten Thema eine E-Mail oder einen Brief. Ganz gleich, welche Art von Text du verfassen musst, die Vorgehensweise ist dabei meist dieselbe.

Arbeitsschritt 1:
Betrachtung/Erfassen

▶ Lies zunächst die Aufgabenstellung beider Schreibaufgaben gut durch und überlege, was jeweils verlangt wird. Obwohl Schwierigkeitsgrad und Umfang gleich sind, solltest du abwägen, welche der beiden Aufgaben dir eher zusagt. Bei der Entscheidung können folgende Fragen helfen:
- Habe ich die Aufgabenstellung einschließlich aller Vorgaben verstanden?
- Habe ich zu dem Thema eigene Ideen und verfüge ich über den nötigen Wortschatz?

Kompetenzbereich: Schreiben 57

▶ Hast du dich für eine der beiden Schreibaufgaben entschieden, geht es an die inhaltliche Planung. Orientiere dich dabei genau an der Aufgabenstellung:

- Markiere die entsprechenden Angaben oder notiere in Stichpunkten, welche Informationen der Text enthalten muss, und überlege, welche eigenen Ideen du einbringen kannst.
- Falls du dich für die Geschichte entschieden hast, überprüfe, ob deine Stichpunktsammlung zu den Vorgaben (z. B. Überschrift) passt.
- Lege die Reihenfolge der Inhalte fest.
- Schlage unbekannten Wortschatz im Wörterbuch nach.
- Berücksichtige Besonderheiten, v. a. wenn du einen formellen Text (z. B. ein Bewerbungsschreiben) verfassen musst.

Arbeitsschritt 2: Brainstorming/Notizen

▶ Arbeite nun deinen Text aus:

- Gliedere deinen Text in Einleitung, Hauptteil und Schluss.
- Greife auf dir bekannte Redemittel / Redewendungen zurück.
- Wähle abwechslungsreiche Satzanfänge und formuliere überschaubare Sätze. Verwende Konjunktionen (z. B. *because, while, after*), um Haupt- und Nebensätze miteinander zu verbinden.
- Verwende die passenden Zeitformen.
- Drücke dich bei formellen E-Mails, z. B. in einem Bewerbungsschreiben, immer höflich aus und verwende die Langformen (z. B. *I am* statt *I'm*). Bei informellen E-Mails, z. B. an eine Freundin, kannst du auch die Kurzformen und umgangssprachliche Formulierungen benutzen.

Arbeitsschritt 3: Verfassen

Auf den Seiten 39–41 haben wir häufig gebrauchte Redewendungen zusammengestellt, die dir beim Formulieren helfen können. Lerne sie auswendig. Zusätzlich hast du die Möglichkeit, viele Redewendungen mithilfe unserer „**MindCards**" interaktiv zu wiederholen. Auf Seite 39 findest du den QR-Code, über den du auf die MindCards zugreifen kannst.

▶ Nimm dir nach Fertigstellung deines Textes Zeit, ihn noch einmal gründlich durchzulesen:

- Hast du alle Vorgaben in der Aufgabenstellung beachtet?
- Sind alle Inhalte (wer, wo, wann, was?) verständlich ausgedrückt?
- Ist dein Text gut gegliedert?
- Sind Gedankensprünge enthalten, die berichtigt werden müssen?
- Hast du häufige Wiederholungen (Inhalt, Wortschatz) vermieden?
- Überlege dir, welche Vokabeln mithilfe des Wörterbuchs auf Bedeutung und/oder Rechtschreibung überprüft werden sollten.

Arbeitsschritt 4: Korrekturlesen

TIPP

- Lies die Aufgabenstellungen genau durch.
- Wähle die für dich geeignete Aufgabe aus.
- Beachte die Vorgaben, die in der Aufgabe genannt werden!
- Erstelle eine Stoffsammlung.
- Arbeite deinen Text sorgfältig aus.
- Lies deinen Text abschließend noch einmal genau durch und überprüfe, ob alles logisch aufgebaut und verständlich geschrieben ist. Verbessere Wortschatz-, Rechtschreib- und Grammatikfehler.

6.2 Hilfreiche Wendungen zur Textproduktion

Anrede und Schlussformeln

Persönlicher Brief/persönliche E-Mail

Liebe Jane,	Dear Jane,
Viele Grüße	Best wishes / Kind regards
Liebe Grüße	Love *(nur bei sehr guten Freunden)*
Mach's gut / Tschüss, Ciao	Take care/Cheers

Formelles Schreiben

wenn du den Namen des Ansprechpartners nicht kennst

Sehr geehrte Damen und Herren,	Dear Sir or Madam,
Mit freundlichen Grüßen	Yours faithfully,

wenn du den Namen des Ansprechpartners kennst

Sehr geehrte Frau Roberts,	Dear Ms / Mrs Roberts,
Sehr geehrter Herr James,	Dear Mr James,
wenn du nicht weißt, ob die Frau verheiratet ist	Dear Ms Bell,
Mit freundlichen Grüßen	Yours sincerely,

Einleitung und Schluss eines Briefes/einer E-Mail

Danke für …	Thank you for …
Ich habe … erhalten.	I (have) received …
Ich hoffe, dass …	I hope that …
Wie geht es dir?	How are you?
In deiner letzten E-Mail hast du mir über … erzählt.	In your last e-mail you told me about …
In deiner letzten E-Mail hast du mir erzählt, dass …	In your last e-mail you told me that …
Entschuldige, dass ich … vergessen habe, aber …	Sorry that I forgot to …, but …
Sage bitte … / Richte … bitte aus …	Please tell …
Es wäre schön, wenn wir uns treffen könnten.	It would be nice if we could meet.
Bitte richte … Grüße aus.	Best wishes to … (Please) give my regards to …
Bitte schreibe mir bald zurück.	Please write soon.
Ich freue mich darauf, bald von dir zu hören.	I'm looking forward to hearing from you. / I hope I'll hear from you soon.

Ich freue mich auf deine E-Mail.	I'm looking / I look forward to your e-mail.
Ich werde dich anrufen.	I'll call you. / I'm going to call you.

Häufig vorkommende Redewendungen/Ausdrücke

sich entschuldigen	I'm sorry
etwas bedauern	It's a pity that … / I'm disappointed that …
an etwas erinnern	Please remember to …
Überraschung äußern	I am/was surprised that …
eine Bitte äußern	Could you/would you …, please?
einen Wunsch äußern	I'd like to …
einen Entschluss mitteilen	I've decided to … I've made up my mind to … I'm going to …
eine Absicht mitteilen	I intend to / I'm planning to … I'm going to / I want to / I will …
Interesse ausdrücken	I'm interested in …
Freude ausdrücken	I'm happy/glad about …
Überzeugung ausdrücken	I'm convinced that … I'm sure that …
nach dem Preis fragen	How much is it? / How much does it cost?
Ich hoffe, dir hat … gefallen.	I hope you liked/enjoyed …
Ich muss jetzt …	I have to …
Ich denke, es ist besser …	I think it's better to …

Auskunft geben über sich selbst

Ich wohne in …	I live in …
Ich wurde am … in … geboren.	I was born on … in …
Ich interessiere mich für …	I'm interested in …
Ich war schon in …	I've (already) been to …
Ich möchte gerne … werden.	I'd like to be / become …
Mir geht es gut.	I'm fine.
Ich mag …	I like … / I enjoy …
Ich mag … lieber (als …).	I prefer to … / I like … better (than …)
Ich weiß … noch nicht genau.	I still don't know exactly …
Ich plane, … zu tun.	I plan to …
Ich freue mich (sehr) auf …	I'm looking forward to … I'm excited about …

Ich konnte ... nicht ...	I wasn't able to ... / I couldn't ...
In meiner Freizeit ...	In my free time/spare time ...
Ich nehme (regelmäßig) an ... teil.	I (regularly) take part in ... / I (regularly) participate in ...

Aufbau eines formellen Briefes

24 Castle Street
Blackburn
Lancashire
LK6 5TQ

> Absender*in (ohne Namen)[1]

6 March 20...

Datum[2]

Mrs J. Fox
Dane Cleaners
3 Arthur Road
Doddington
NE3 6LD

> Empfänger*in (nur in formellen Briefen)

Dear Mrs Fox,

Anrede

Thank you for your letter ...

Brief

Yours sincerely,

Schlussformel

Adam Smith

Unterschrift

Adam Smith

Name

1 Die Adresse des Absenders kann auch auf der linken Seite stehen
2 *Auch möglich: 6th March 20... oder March 6, 20...; das Datum kann auch links stehen*

6.3 Übungsaufgaben zum Kompetenzbereich „Schreiben"

Hier findest du zahlreiche Aufgaben zum Bereich „Schreiben". In den Übersichtskästen kannst du nachlesen, worauf es in den folgenden Aufgaben ankommt bzw. was von dir erwartet wird.

TIPP

> *Sprachliche Ausdrucksfähigkeit*
> - Beim Schreiben von Texten kommt es darauf an, dass du deine Sätze **sprachlich variieren** kannst. Wiederholungen derselben Ausdrücke und Satzmuster sind langweilig.
> - Außerdem ist es sinnvoll, Haupt- und Nebensätze miteinander zu verknüpfen, um z. B. Auswirkungen oder Folgen zu verdeutlichen. Diese Verknüpfungen können durch entsprechende **Bindewörter** (Konjunktionen) hergestellt werden.
>
> In den folgenden beiden Aufgaben kannst du diese zwei Punkte gezielt üben. Versuche auch bei allen weiteren Schreibaufgaben, auf sprachliche Variation bzw. auf die Verknüpfung von Sätzen durch Konjunktionen zu achten.

1. Sieh dir diesen Satz an: *The old house at the end of the street is ours.*

    Wandle ihn nun ab, indem du die folgenden Sätze ergänzt.

    Beispiel: We live _____.

    We live *in the old house at the end of the street.*

    a) I like _____, which _____.

    b) At the end of _____ you find _____.

    c) The street ends where _____.

    d) Do you know the house _____?

    It's _____.

    e) Our _____ is _____ and at _____.

2. Wähle die passenden Konjunktionen, um die Haupt- und Nebensätze zu verbinden. Es sind mehr Wörter vorgegeben, als du brauchst.

after • when • while • if • because • that • so • but • although • and • as

    a) _____ I left the house this morning I noticed that I had left behind my umbrella.

    b) I would have needed it _____ it started to rain.

    c) _____ I did not want to get wet I took the bus.

    d) _____ I got off the bus, it was still raining.

    e) It rained so heavily _____ I got completely wet.

    f) _____ I drank a cup of hot tea in the office, I was ill the next day _____ had to stay in bed.

TIPP

Bilder als Schreibanlässe

In der schriftlichen Abschlussprüfung kannst du dich im Bereich Schreiben – *Creative Writing* auf folgende Aufgabentypen einstellen:

- **Picture and Prompts:** Du verfasst eine Geschichte zu einem Bild. Dabei sind zusätzlich **Stichwörter** (*prompts*) auf Deutsch vorgegeben.
- **Picture Story:** Hier musst du eine **Bildergeschichte** schreiben.

In beiden Fällen dient das Bildmaterial als Grundlage für deinen Text. Das Ergebnis soll keine reine Bildbeschreibung sein, sondern eine Geschichte, in der die Bilder berücksichtigt wurden.

Picture and prompts

Die folgenden Schritte helfen dir, eine gelungene Geschichte zu einem Bild und den dazugehörigen Stichwörtern zu schreiben.

Schritt 1: Betrachtung

Betrachte das Bild genau. Lies die deutschen Stichwörter dazu und gegebenenfalls den Satzanfang. Überlege, wie die Stichwörter und das Bild zusammenhängen. Denke dir eine Handlung aus, die sich aufgrund der Informationen sowohl aus dem Bild als auch aus den Stichwörtern ergeben könnte.

Schritt 2: Brainstorming

Wähle die Ideen aus, die du in deiner Geschichte verwenden möchtest. Du kannst die Notizen auch erst auf Deutsch erstellen und sie anschließend übersetzen. Verwende bei Bedarf ein Wörterbuch.

Schritt 3: Verfassen

Schreibe nun eine Geschichte im vorgeschriebenen Umfang. Überlege dir bei der Ausformulierung, was in die oftmals vorgegebene Einleitung, in den Hauptteil (Spannungsbogen) und in den Schluss gehört. Entscheide, welchen Inhalt du besonders ausgestalten möchtest, beispielsweise als Höhepunkt der Geschichte. Verwende bei Bedarf ein Wörterbuch. Wähle auch die richtige Zeitform: eine Geschichte schreibst du meist in der Vergangenheit (*simple past*). Der vorgegebene Satzanfang gibt die Haupt-Zeitform vor, z. B. *Last year we went to …*

Schritt 4: Korrekturlesen

Überprüfe deine Geschichte, indem du sie noch einmal daraufhin durchliest, ob folgende Punkte erfüllt sind:

- Gibt es eine Einleitung, einen Hauptteil und einen Schluss?
- Sind alle wichtigen Informationen enthalten (wer, wo, was, wann)? Vergleiche mit dem Bild und den Stichwörtern.
- Ist der Text verständlich, auch wenn man die Vorgaben und das Bild / die Bilder nicht kennt?

Anhand der folgenden Aufgaben kannst du diese Schritte anwenden. Zu Beginn werden dir noch viele Hinweise gegeben. Dann werden die Hilfen immer weniger, sodass die Aufgaben immer mehr denjenigen in der Prüfung entsprechen.

3. Sieh dir das Foto mit den Stichwörtern *(prompts)* an und bearbeite die Aufgaben.

© Gareth Boden. Pearson Education Ltd.

a) Wähle aus der folgenden Liste Ideen für deine Geschichte aus.
   - a juggler was giving a performance
   - he dropped one of his clubs
   - the juggler asked the people for some coins
   - the juggler asked: "Would you like to try juggling, too?"
   - the spectators *(Zuschauer*innen)* were asked to try juggling
   - the wind blew the hat off the juggler's head
   - the juggler's suitcase was stolen
   - the young woman's handbag was stolen
   - when the juggler opened his suitcase: what was inside?

b) Wähle Wörter aus, die du in deiner Geschichte verwenden könntest. Du kannst natürlich auch Wörter nehmen, die hier nicht aufgeführt sind.

   Place (location): town / city centre / market square / street cafés / pedestrian zone

   Characters: artist / juggler / (young) man / young woman with bag / three friends / policeman / passers-by: tourists / locals / friends

   Clothes/Gadgets: suit / clubs / hat / mobile phone / suitcase / bag

   Actions: juggle / watch / buy / go shopping / go sightseeing / collect money / fall down / drop / steal

   Emotions: sad / happy / shocked / surprised / frightened / excited / impressed / nervous

   Connecting words: suddenly / because / while / when / after / because / then

Kompetenzbereich: Schreiben

c) Verwende deine Ideen und den von dir ausgewählten Wortschatz, um eine Geschichte von mindestens 100 Wörtern auf Englisch zu schreiben, in der du das Bild sowie die deutschen Angaben berücksichtigst. Versuche auch, wörtliche Rede einzubauen: Was könnten die Personen sagen, denken oder fühlen? Sieh dir auch noch einmal die einzelnen Schritte auf S. 43 an.

Beginne wie folgt:

What a surprise!

On a Saturday afternoon, Lisa was …

Kompetenzbereich: Schreiben | 65

4. *Hitchhiking Picture and prompts 1:* Verfasse eine Geschichte von mindestens 100 Wörtern, in der du das Bild *(picture)* und die Stichwörter *(prompts)* berücksichtigst. Betrachte zuerst das Foto und lies die dazugehörigen Angaben. Beachte auch die Überschrift sowie den Satzanfang.

Summer trip

Last August, …

© abadesign. Shutterstock

a) Mache dir Notizen (Brainstorming).

_____
_____
_____
_____

b) Verfasse nun mithilfe deiner Notizen eine Geschichte. Vergiss am Ende das Korrekturlesen nicht.

_____
_____
_____
_____
_____
_____
_____
_____

5. *Hitchhiking Picture and prompts 2:* Sieh dir das Bild und die Stichwörter an. Mache dir zuerst Notizen auf ein separates Blatt und verfasse dann eine Geschichte, in der du die Zeichnung und die Angaben berücksichtigst. Verwende auch die wörtliche Rede: Was könnten die Personen sagen, denken und fühlen? Sieh dir auch noch einmal die einzelnen Schritte auf S. 43 an. Schreibe mindestens 100 Wörter und beginne wie folgt:

A trip to remember!

© Rebecca Meyer

The day before St. Patrick's Day, Tina and Tom wanted to hitchhike to ...

Kompetenzbereich: Schreiben | 67

TIPP

Picture story

Die folgenden Schritte helfen dir, eine gelungene **Bildergeschichte** zu schreiben.

Schritt 1: Betrachtung

Sieh dir die Bilder der Geschichte genau an, um zu verstehen, worum es geht. Manchmal findest du zu den Bildern auch Hinweise, z. B. in Form von Sprechblasen oder Bildtiteln.

Schritt 2: Brainstorming

Überlege, was unbedingt in die Geschichte gehört und halte dies mit Stichpunkten fest. Verwende gegebenenfalls das Wörterbuch. Achte darauf, dass die Stichpunkte inhaltlich zur vorgegebenen Überschrift passen.

Schritt 3: Verfassen

Schreibe nun deine Geschichte. Beachte den vorgeschriebenen Umfang (mind. 100 Wörter). Wähle die richtige Zeitform: Meist schreibst du eine Geschichte im „Simple past". Der Anfang der Geschichte gibt die Zeitform vor. Verwende bei Bedarf ein Wörterbuch (du kannst hier auch die Vergangenheitsform der Verben nachschlagen). Überlege dir eine Einleitung, den Hauptteil (Spannungsbogen) und einen passenden Schluss. Entscheide, wie du den Höhepunkt der Geschichte besonders ausgestalten könntest (z. B. mit wörtlicher Rede).

Schritt 4: Korrekturlesen

Überprüfe deine Geschichte, indem du sie noch einmal daraufhin durchliest, ob der Text logisch aufgebaut und verständlich ist, auch wenn man die Bilder nicht kennt.

6. Verwende die folgenden Bilder für eine Geschichte. Halte dich dabei an den vorgegebenen Anfang und überlege dir ein interessantes Ende. Schreibe mindestens 100 Wörter.

A banana in the way

Luke was taking a walk in the park when he received a message from …

© Maridav. Shutterstock, © ESUN7756. Shutterstock, © Georgios Kollidas. Shutterstock

Kompetenzbereich: Schreiben

7. Sieh dir die einzelnen Bilder genau an und verwende ungefähr 100 Wörter, um die Bildergeschichte auf Englisch zu erzählen. Lies auch noch einmal die einzelnen Schritte auf S. 48 durch. Beginne wie folgt:

The suspect

At teatime Mr Smith wanted to have some biscuits ...

Illustrationen: © Bernd Wiedemann

Kompetenzbereich: Schreiben | 69

8. Sieh dir die einzelnen Bilder genau an und verwende mindestens 100 Wörter, um die Bildergeschichte auf Englisch zu erzählen. Lies auch noch einmal die einzelnen Schritte auf S. 48 durch. Beginne wie folgt:

One stop too far

On Saturday evening, Jenny got on the train ...

Illustrationen: © Rebecca Meyer

70 | **Kompetenzbereich: Schreiben**

TIPP

Correspondence

In der schriftlichen Abschlussprüfung kannst du dich in diesem Bereich auf folgende Aufgaben-typen einstellen:

- **persönliche E-Mail/persönlicher Brief**, z. B. an Freunde oder die Familie
- **formelle E-Mail/formeller Brief**, z. B. Bewerbung/Lebenslauf

Du bekommst inhaltliche Vorgaben, die du mit Beispielen sowie mit eigenen Ideen ausge-stalten sollst. Es wird keine wörtliche Übersetzung der Vorgaben erwartet. Die folgenden Schritte helfen dir, einen gelungenen Text zu schreiben.

Schritt 1: Erfassen der Aufgabenstellung

Beginne, indem du die Aufgabe gründlich durchliest. Markiere wichtige Informationen. Kläre, an wen dein Anschreiben gerichtet ist (z. B. an einen Freund oder eine Mitarbeiterin einer Personalabteilung), bzw. welchen Zweck das Anschreiben hat (z. B. Kennenlernen einer Brief-freundin oder Bewerbung um einen Ferienjob).

Schritt 2: Notizen

Notiere dir auf Grundlage der Angaben, welche Inhalte unbedingt in deine E-Mail/deinen Brief gehören. Falls die Aufgabenstellung ein Schreiben enthält, das es zu beantworten gilt, solltest du dir Antworten zu den dort gestellten Fragen notieren. Formuliere auch eigene Fragen an den Absender/die Absenderin. Überlege dir, wie du die vorgegebenen Inhalte durch eigene Ideen ergänzen kannst. Wenn es dir hilft, kannst du diese Notizen zunächst auf Deutsch er-stellen und anschließend übersetzen. Verwende bei Bedarf das Wörterbuch.

Schritt 3: Verfassen

Beachte dabei den vorgeschriebenen Umfang (in der Prüfung ca. 100 Wörter oder auch mehr). Verwende bei Bedarf ein Wörterbuch. Überlege, welche Zeitform du verwenden musst, und in welcher Reihenfolge du die Inhalte präsentierst. Achte auch auf formale Kriterien wie Da-tum, Anrede, Schlussformel oder die tabellarische Form beim Lebenslauf.

Tipp: Am einfachsten ist es, wenn du beim Datum folgende Variante wählst:

> z. B. *1 November 20…* / *19 March 20…*

Schritt 4: Korrekturlesen

Lies deinen Text zum Schluss noch einmal durch. Hast du alle Vorgaben beachtet?

- Werden die formalen Kriterien erfüllt (z. B. Datum, Anrede, Schlussformel)?
- Sind alle wichtigen Informationen enthalten?
- Ist der Text sauber und leserlich verfasst?
- Hast du die richtigen Zeitformen verwendet?

Die folgenden Übungen führen dich Schritt für Schritt an die oben beschriebene Arbeitsweise heran, sodass du am Schluss Aufgaben bearbeiten kannst, die dem Niveau des Quali entsprechen.

9. Nach dem Schulabschluss planst du, für drei Monate nach Ontario (Provinz in Kanada) zu gehen. Jessy ist die Tochter deiner künftigen Gastfamilie und ihr tauscht seit Kurzem Textnachrichten aus. Ergänze folgenden Dialog auf Englisch. Beachte, dass es zwischen Deutschland und Ontario eine Zeitver-schiebung von sechs Stunden gibt.

Jessy: Hi! Sorry for writing late. I'm just on my way to school. TGIF! How was your day?

Kompetenzbereich: Schreiben | 71

Du: *Schildere deinen Tagesablauf. Erzähle von deinen Erlebnissen in der Schule und was du heute noch machen wirst.*

Jessy: You're sooo lucky that you're already done with school for this week! My friend's having a sleepover party at her house tonight. Not sure if I'll go there, though. I don't feel well. What are your plans for the weekend?

Du: *Beantworte Jessys Frage, indem du von deinen Plänen für das Wochenende berichtest.*

Jessy: Sounds great! You know, it's going to be so much fun once you come over to stay with us! By the way, my mom wants to know if there is any food that you don't like???

Du: *Informiere Jessy über deine Essgewohnheiten. Gibt es bestimmte Lebensmittel, die du nicht essen kannst/willst? Mache einen Vorschlag, was ihr zusammen kochen könnt, und begründe, warum du gerade dieses Gericht vorschlägst.*

Jessy: Sounds yummy! Anything else you'd like to know?

Du: *Stelle Jessy Fragen über deinen Aufenthalt, z. B. deine Unterbringung, den Besuch eines Sprachkurses, Freizeitmöglichkeiten, eine Geschenkidee für ihre Eltern …*

Jessy: Sorry! Have to get back to you later on all of that. We just arrived at school. Bye!

Kompetenzbereich: Schreiben

10. Du verbringst zusammen mit deinen Eltern einen Urlaub in Südafrika und schreibst deiner Lieblingstante Emily, die Engländerin ist, eine Postkarte. Ihr habt viele Programmpunkte. Ergänze den folgenden Text mithilfe der Angaben.

   ▶ *Ankunft in Kapstadt (Cape Town)*
   ▶ *Entspannen im Hotel und am Strand*
   ▶ *Besichtigung von Kapstadt und Einkaufsbummel in der City*
   ▶ *Wanderung zum Lion's Head: toller Ausblick auf die Stadt und das Meer*
   ▶ *Besuch eines Surfkurses an der False Bay*
   ▶ *Flug von Kapstadt nach Johannesburg*
   ▶ *Barbecue und Übernachtung in einer Lodge im Kruger National Park, Safari am nächsten Tag, um wilde Tiere zu beobachten.*
   ▶ *Rückflug nach Deutschland*

© Matej Kastelic. Shutterstock

_____ (date)

_____ Emily,

Best _____ from Johannesburg! I'm here with _____.
This place is _____! The weather is
_____ and I'm feeling
_____.

This is what we've already done in our holidays:
_____
_____
_____
_____
_____

And we have further plans:
_____
_____
_____
_____
_____

☐ Love,   ☐ Regards,   *(tick the box with the suitable ending)*

_____

11. Lies folgende E-Mail von deinem Freund Sean aus Dublin:

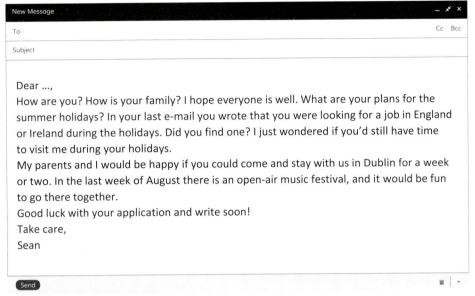

Dear ...,
How are you? How is your family? I hope everyone is well. What are your plans for the summer holidays? In your last e-mail you wrote that you were looking for a job in England or Ireland during the holidays. Did you find one? I just wondered if you'd still have time to visit me during your holidays.
My parents and I would be happy if you could come and stay with us in Dublin for a week or two. In the last week of August there is an open-air music festival, and it would be fun to go there together.
Good luck with your application and write soon!
Take care,
Sean

E-Mail-Maske © designmaestro. Shutterstock

Antworte ihm auf Englisch und verwende dabei die aufgelisteten Vorgaben. Schreibe mindestens 100 Wörter. Du kannst dir auch noch einmal die einzelnen Schritte zum Verfassen einer E-Mail auf S. 51 ansehen.

- *Bedanke dich für Seans E-Mail.*
- *Erzähle Sean, dass du einen Ferienjob in einem Hotel bekommen hast.*
- *Erkläre, bei welchen Tätigkeiten du im Hotel helfen wirst: z. B. Zimmer aufräumen und die Betten machen, Mithilfe in der Küche, Pflege des Hotelgartens*
- *Schreibe Sean, ob du ihn besuchen wirst oder nicht, und begründe deine Entscheidung.*
- *Denke an eine angemessene Begrüßung und Verabschiedung.*

Kompetenzbereich: Schreiben

12. Deine Brieffreundin Vanessa aus Australien hat derzeit Schulferien. Sie macht ein Praktikum in einer Auffangstation für Wildtiere. Du erhältst folgende Nachricht von ihr:

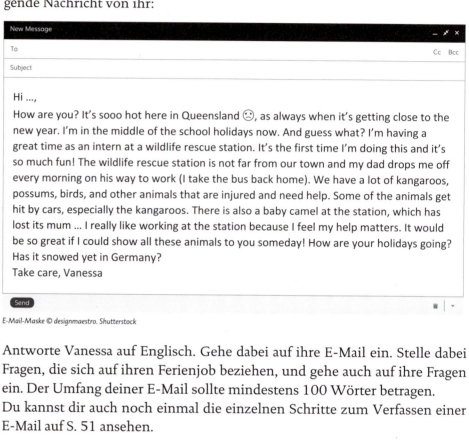

Hi …,

How are you? It's sooo hot here in Queensland ☹, as always when it's getting close to the new year. I'm in the middle of the school holidays now. And guess what? I'm having a great time as an intern at a wildlife rescue station. It's the first time I'm doing this and it's so much fun! The wildlife rescue station is not far from our town and my dad drops me off every morning on his way to work (I take the bus back home). We have a lot of kangaroos, possums, birds, and other animals that are injured and need help. Some of the animals get hit by cars, especially the kangaroos. There is also a baby camel at the station, which has lost its mum … I really like working at the station because I feel my help matters. It would be so great if I could show all these animals to you someday! How are your holidays going? Has it snowed yet in Germany?
Take care, Vanessa

E-Mail-Maske © designmaestro. Shutterstock

Antworte Vanessa auf Englisch. Gehe dabei auf ihre E-Mail ein. Stelle dabei Fragen, die sich auf ihren Ferienjob beziehen, und gehe auch auf ihre Fragen ein. Der Umfang deiner E-Mail sollte mindestens 100 Wörter betragen.
Du kannst dir auch noch einmal die einzelnen Schritte zum Verfassen einer E-Mail auf S. 51 ansehen.

Kompetenzbereich: Schreiben | 75

13. Du möchtest in den Sommerferien ein wenig Geld verdienen und außerdem ein anderes Land kennenlernen. Im Internet findest du folgende Stellenanzeige für einen Ferienjob in einem Hotel in Brighton, England. Lies dir folgende Anzeige gut durch.

OCEANVIEW HOTEL

First-class hotel
is looking for
temporary personnel
for the summer.
Customer skills necessary
Send a CV and a letter of application to Mr Tom Leary
Oceanview Hotel, 21 Seafront Road, Brighton BN3 6AB

Bild Hotel © Can Stock Photo/styf22

a) Fülle das Online-Bewerbungsformular aus.

Name: _____ (first) _____ (last)

Gender: ☐ female   ☐ male   ☐ other

Date of birth: _____

Nationality: _____

E-Mail: _____

Position you want to apply for:
☐ receptionist   ☐ room service   ☐ kitchen help

Availability:
From: _____ (day) _____ (month) _____ (year)
To: _____ (day) _____ (month) _____ (year)

How many hours do you want to work per week?
☐ under 10   ☐ 10 – 20   ☐ 20 – 30   ☐ over 30

Preferred working period: ☐ mornings   ☐ afternoons   ☐ evenings

Do you have a valid driver's licence? ☐ yes   ☐ no

Languages spoken: ☐ English   ☐ French   ☐ Spanish
                    ☐ Others: _____

Current occupation: ☐ student   ☐ apprentice   ☐ employed   ☐ unemployed

Work experience:

_____

What makes you a true Oceanview Hotel staff member? I am …

☐ hard-working   ☐ open-minded   ☐ friendly   ☐ helpful
☐ independent   ☐ flexible   ☐ ready to learn ☐ reliable
☐ skilful   ☐ clever   ☐ communicative   ☐ sociable

76 / **Kompetenzbereich: Schreiben**

b) Vervollständige nun dein Bewerbungsschreiben für den Ferienjob in dem Hotel in England.

_____,

(Anrede)

I saw your job advert _____ and I'm interested in working at _____.

My name is _____, I am _____ old and live in _____, Germany.

I am graduating from school in _____. I have been learning English for _____ years and can speak it _____.

During my last summer holidays I _____

_____.

I am the right person for the job because _____

_____.

Working at your hotel would be a great opportunity for me to

_____.

Could you please give me some more information about the job?

How long _____?

How much _____?

I look forward _____.

_____

(Schluss)

_____

(Name)

14. Du willst im Rahmen des „Work and Travel"-Programms für ein Jahr nach Australien gehen. So kannst du das Land kennenlernen und dabei Geld verdienen. Eine Agentur empfiehlt, dass du dich zunächst als Bedienung in einem Café in Margaret River, Western Australia, bewirbst. Wende dich an Mrs Jackson, die als Ansprechpartnerin des „River Cafés" genannt wird. Du kannst dir auch noch einmal die einzelnen Schritte zum Verfassen einer E-Mail auf S. 51 ansehen.

a) Verfasse das Anschreiben. Schreibe mindestens 100 Wörter und gehe dabei auf folgende Punkte ein:

▶ *Auf welche Stelle bewirbst du dich?*
▶ *Wie bist du auf die Stelle aufmerksam geworden?*
▶ *Stelle dich kurz vor.*
▶ *Nenne Gründe, warum du dich für die Stelle interessierst.*
▶ *Gib an, in welchem Zeitraum du arbeiten könntest.*

Kompetenzbereich: Schreiben 77

▶ *Begründe, warum du für den Job geeignet bist.*
▶ *Erkundige dich nach Arbeitszeiten und Gehalt.*

b) Verfasse einen tabellarischen Lebenslauf, in dem du folgende Punkte berücksichtigst. Schreibe mindestens 30 Wörter.

▶ *Angaben zu deiner Person (Vor- und Nachname, Geburtsdatum und -ort)*
▶ *Angaben zu deinem Schulabschluss und deiner Ausbildung*
▶ *Praktische Erfahrungen*
▶ *Besondere Fertigkeiten („skills") und persönliche Interessen*

7 Kompetenzbereich: Sprechen

Die **mündliche Prüfung** im Fach Englisch wird von der Schule gestellt, an der du den Quali ablegst. Aus diesem Grund kann die Prüfung von Schule zu Schule verschieden sein. Einheitlich ist jedoch die Arbeitszeit – sie beträgt 15 Minuten pro Schüler/in. Erkundige dich rechtzeitig bei der zuständigen Lehrkraft nach den Prüfungsanforderungen.

7.1 Hinweise und Strategien zum Kompetenzbereich „Sprechen"

Indem du den Quali im Fach Englisch ablegst, beweist du, dass du über bestimmte sprachliche Fähigkeiten verfügst. Deine Fähigkeiten entsprechen den Anforderungen des Niveaus A2/A2+, die in einem gemeinsamen Europäischen Standard *(Common European Framework of Reference)* festgelegt sind. Damit festgestellt werden kann, ob du dieses Niveau erreicht hast, enthält die mündliche Prüfung im Fach Englisch an den meisten Schulen folgende Prüfungsteile:

Ablauf der Prüfung

▶ Die Prüfung beginnt mit dem „**Opening talk**". Das ist ein **einleitendes Gespräch**, das nicht bewertet wird. Die prüfende Lehrkraft begrüßt dich und stellt dir einige kurze Fragen auf Englisch. Auf diese Weise kannst du dich leichter in die Prüfungssituation einfinden.
Mögliche Fragen könnten sein:
- How are you? *(Wie geht es dir?)*
- Are you very excited? *(Bist du sehr aufgeregt?)*
- What did you do this morning? *(Was hast du heute Morgen gemacht?)*
- Do you have any questions before the exam starts?
  (Hast du noch Fragen, bevor die Prüfung anfängt?)

Daran können sich verschiedene Prüfungsteile anschließen:

▶ „**Picture-based interview**": Dies ist ein Gespräch auf Grundlage eines Bildes, das dir vorgelegt wird. Zunächst werden Fragen gestellt, die sich direkt auf das Bild beziehen. Es folgen dann weitere Fragen an dich, die über den Bildinhalt hinausgehen.

▶ „**Topic-based talk**": Du erhältst eine **Mindmap** zu einem landeskundlichen oder allgemeinen Thema. Aus den Stichwörtern der Mindmap wählst du **drei** aus. Anschließend sprichst du in einem kurzen Vortrag etwa 2 Minuten lang zu diesen Punkten.

▶ **Sprachmittlung:** In diesem Prüfungsteil dolmetscht du in einem Gespräch zwischen einem englischen *native speaker* und einem/einer Deutschen. Falls möglich, solltet ihr euch zu viert auf die Sprachmittlung vorbereiten. Zwei Mitschüler/innen können den Dialog vortragen, während der/die Dritte dolmetscht. Die vierte Person beobachtet euch und gibt im Anschluss eine Rückmeldung, z. B. zum Sprechtempo und zur Aussprache, und macht Verbesserungsvorschläge (z. B. im Bereich Wortschatz und Grammatik). Falls du alleine übst, kannst du das Gespräch aufzeichnen (denke an Pausen, die du zum Übersetzen brauchst) und anschließend dolmetschen. Vergleiche deine Lösung in einem zweiten Durchlauf Satz für Satz mit der Musterlösung. Beachte aber, dass es häufig mehrere richtige Lösungen gibt, die vielleicht nicht angegeben sind. Es ist auf jeden Fall **hilfreich**, sich vorher **Situationen zu überlegen**, in denen man dolmetschen müsste, wie z. B. beim Einkaufen oder im Hotel. So kann man sich schon einmal Vokabeln und Wendungen dazu überlegen.

▶ **„Reacting to prompts"**: Du erhältst eine Karte, auf der eine Situation und deine Rolle beschrieben sind. Außerdem findest du darauf einige Stichwörter in englischer Sprache, die zur Situation/Rolle passen. Je nach Aufgabenstellung baust du nun diese Stichwörter in einen kurzen Vortrag zum Thema ein, oder aber du verwendest diese in einem Dialog mit der Lehrkraft, die mit dir ein Gespräch zu deinem Thema führen wird.

▶ **„Oral report"** (Referat mit anschließenden Fragen): Beim *Oral report* bereitest du nach Rücksprache mit der zuständigen Schule ein Referat vor, das du in der mündlichen Prüfung vorträgst, und zu dem dir auch Fragen gestellt werden. Das Referat muss frei gehalten werden, d. h., du sollst deinen ausgearbeiteten Vortrag **nicht** vom Blatt ablesen. Als Hilfestellung in der Prüfung können dir Stichpunkte oder auch eine Mindmap dienen.

Im Unterschied zum *Topic-based talk* steht dir für den *Oral report* üblicherweise eine längere Vorbereitungszeit zur Verfügung. Da beim *Oral report* jedoch nur das Thema vorgegeben ist, bist du für die inhaltliche Ausgestaltung deines Referats selbst verantwortlich. Du erhältst also im Gegensatz zum *Topic-based talk* **keine Mindmap**, die dir als Leitfaden dient. Die Tipps, die in diesem Buch für den *Topic-based talk* enthalten sind, können aber auch für den *Oral report* hilfreich sein.

Das Ende der Prüfung signalisiert ein kurzes Abschlussgespräch, mit dem du aus der Prüfungssituation entlassen wirst. Dieses fließt, wie der *Opening talk*, nicht in die Bewertung ein.

Da der mündliche Englisch-Quali nur 15 Minuten dauert, werden nicht alle genannten Teile geprüft. Die Schule entscheidet über die Zusammenstellung der Prüfung, indem sie meist **drei Prüfungsteile** auswählt, also z. B. das *Picture-based interview*, den *Topic-based talk* und die Sprachmittlung.

Deine **Note** in der mündlichen Prüfung wird anhand eines Notenschlüssels ermittelt. Die sprachliche Leistung steht dabei im Mittelpunkt, es wird aber z. B. auch darauf geachtet, ob du auf die Fragen der Prüfer eingehst, ob du Ideen und Informationen flüssig und verständlich zum Ausdruck bringst, oder ob du erlernte Strategien angewendet hast, indem du beispielsweise einen Begriff umschreibst, wenn dir das entsprechende englische Wort nicht einfällt.

7.2 Hilfreiche Wendungen und Beispiele zum Kompetenzbereich „Sprechen"

Diese Aufforderungen und Fragen können im Prüfungsteil „**Picture-based interview**" an dich gerichtet werden:

Sieh dir das Bild an.	Look at the picture.
Beschreibe die Szene.	Describe the scene.
Beschreibe, was du siehst.	Describe what you see.
Was denkst du über …?	What do you think about …?
Was hältst du von …?	What's your opinion about …?
Sprich über…	Talk about …
Berichte mir über …	Tell me about …
Erkläre, warum …	Explain why …
Würdest du gerne über … sprechen?	Would you like to discuss …?

Hilfreiche Wendungen für den Prüfungsteil „**Picture-based interview**":

Dieses Bild zeigt/stellt dar …	This picture shows …
Es gibt …	There is/are …
Ich kann/wir können … im Bild sehen.	I/we can see … in the picture.
oben/unten im Bild …	At the top/at the bottom of the picture …
links/rechts …	On the left/right hand side …
Im Vordergrund/Hintergrund …	In the foreground/background …

Hilfreiche Wendungen für den Prüfungsteil „**Topic-based talk**":

Mein Thema ist …	My topic/subject is …
Ich habe folgende Punkte ausgewählt: …	I chose these aspects/keywords: …
Ich möchte über das folgende Thema sprechen: …	I'd like to talk about this aspect/subject/keyword: …
Ich werde mich auf folgende Bereiche konzentrieren: …	I'm going to concentrate on the following issues: …
Ich möchte/werde über … sprechen.	I'd like to/I'm going to talk about … / The topic of my talk is …
Zuerst …, dann …, später …	First …, then …, afterwards …
Mein erster/zweiter/dritter/letzter Punkt ist …	My first/second/third/last point is …
Am Ende/Abschließend will ich über … sprechen.	Finally, I'm going to talk about … / To finish, I'm going to talk about …

Kompetenzbereich: Sprechen

Hier folgen ein paar Beispiele für typische Alltagssituationen für den Prüfungsteil „**Sprachmittlung**":

Im Hotel	At the hotel
Im Souvenirgeschäft	At the souvenir shop
Am Telefon	On the telephone
In einem Restaurant	In a restaurant
Am Bahnhof	At the station
Nach dem Weg fragen	Asking the way
Im Fremdenverkehrsamt/ In der Touristeninformation	At the tourist information centre
Im Reisebüro	At the travel agent's

Hilfreiche Wendungen für den Prüfungsteil „**Sprachmittlung**":

Entschuldigung, ich habe Sie nicht verstanden.	Sorry, I didn't understand/get you.
Könnten Sie bitte langsamer sprechen?	Could you speak more slowly, please?
Könnten Sie das bitte wiederholen?	Could you please repeat that?
Könnten Sie mir bitte erklären, was … ist?	Could you please explain what (a) … is?
Könnten Sie mir bitte das Wort … erklären?	Could you please explain the word … to me?
Was meinen Sie, wenn Sie … sagen?	What do you mean when you say …?

Seine **Meinung** äußern/seine Einschätzung zum Ausdruck bringen:

Meiner Meinung nach …	In my opinion … / I think/believe that …
Ich kann/könnte mir vorstellen, dass …	I can/could imagine that …
Ich würde (nicht) gerne …	I would/wouldn't like to …
Ich bevorzuge …	I prefer …
Ich mag … lieber als …	I like … better than …
Ich stimme zu, dass … / Ich stimme nicht zu, dass …	I agree that … / I disagree that …
Ich kann/könnte mir vorstellen, dass …	I can/could imagine that …

Die hilfreichen Wendungen auf Seite 61/62, und einige mehr, kannst du mithilfe unserer App „**MindCards**" interaktiv wiederholen. Verwende dazu den nebenstehenden QR-Code.

7.3 Übungsaufgaben zum Kompetenzbereich „Sprechen"

TIPP

Picture-based interview

Dieser Prüfungsteil dauert im Regelfall rund 5 Minuten. Es wird dir dabei ein Bild vorgelegt. Nachdem du es betrachtet hast, werden dir gezielt einige Fragen zum Bild als Ganzes oder zu einem Ausschnitt gestellt.

Wenn du beschreiben willst, welche Szene auf dem Foto dargestellt ist, verwendest du als Zeitform üblicherweise das *present progressive*. Damit drückst du aus, was gerade geschieht, oder was jemand gerade tut.

Beispiel:

Aussagesatz: He is playing the keyboard.
Verneinung: He isn't singing.

Ausgehend vom Bild werden dir nun noch weiterführende Fragen gestellt, bei denen es häufig um deine persönliche Meinung, Erfahrung oder Einschätzung geht. Beantworte diese Fragen ausführlich, indem du deine Antworten begründest. Als Zeitform wird hier überwiegend das *simple present* zum Einsatz kommen, das man bei allgemeingültigen Aussagen oder auch bei Tätigkeiten, die man häufig ausführt, verwendet.

Beispiel:

Aussagesatz: I play the guitar.
Verneinung: I don't practice every day.

Worksheet

1. Foto: „Music band"

© Nejron/Dreamstime.com

Look at the picture for 30 seconds before you read the task.
Now talk about the following aspects for 3 minutes:

a) Talk about the place.
b) Describe what the people are doing.
c) Describe their clothes.
d) Do you think it is more fun to make music alone or in a group? Give reasons.
e) What type of music do you like? Why?

2. Foto: „Chicken man"

© Gareth Boden. Pearson Education Ltd

Look at the picture for 30 seconds before you read the task.
Now talk about the following aspects for 3 minutes:

- a) What are the two people in the picture doing?
- b) Describe what each of them is wearing.
- c) What is the weather in this scene like?
- d) Why do you think the man is wearing a costume?
- e) Do you like watching street artists? Why?/Why not?

3. Foto: „Young people and digital media"

© viewapart. 123rf.com

Look at the picture for 30 seconds before you read the task.
Now talk about the following aspects for 3 minutes:

a) Describe where the teenagers are.
b) Talk about the things or gadgets these young people have with them.
c) Are the people in this photo communicating with each other? Why/ Why not?
d) Do you think the people in this group are friends? Give reasons.
e) In your opinion, is it better to meet friends in person or to communicate with them online? Why?/Why not?

4. Video: „Superhero"

   Watch the video clip using the following link:

   http://qrcode.stark-verlag.de/93555

   or the QR-Code:

   Toyota Motor Corporation Australia Ltd

   Then describe in only a few words what you have seen.
   Now answer these questions:

   a) Why does the man desperately want to reach his car?
   b) Why does his daughter show him her doll's foot?
   c) How do you think the father feels after he sees where the doll's shoe is?
   d) Do you think that the father is like a superhero? Why?
   e) Why do you think the commercial suggests that the car is "for real superheros"?

Topic-based talk

Hier wird von dir erwartet, einen **kurzen Vortrag** zu halten. Diesen Vortrag bereitest und trägst du **direkt** in der Prüfung vor. Dazu erhältst du eine **Mindmap** mit Stichwörtern zu einem alltäglichen Thema oder zu einem englischsprachigen Land. Es ist von Vorteil, wenn du bereits inhaltliche Vorkenntnisse hast, aber mithilfe der Stichwörter sollte es dir immer möglich sein, einen guten Text zu formulieren.

- Nachdem dir die Mindmap vorgelegt wurde, wählst du aus den angegebenen Punkten nur diejenigen **3 Aspekte** aus, zu denen dir am meisten einfällt. Du hast nun ca. 90 Sekunden Zeit, dir zu überlegen, was du zu den Punkten sagen kannst, bevor dein Vortrag beginnt.
- Achte auf einen schlüssigen Vortrag: Die Informationen müssen zum Thema passen und von den Prüfern inhaltlich zugeordnet und verstanden werden können. Vermeide Überschneidungen; das gelingt, wenn du zu jedem Aspekt neue Informationen gibst und bereits Gesagtes nicht wiederholst.
- Deine Redezeit beträgt insgesamt rund **2 Minuten**. Mache dir keine Sorgen, falls dein Vortrag kürzer ausfällt. Die Prüfer werden dir in diesem Fall noch einige Fragen zum Thema stellen, z. B. "Would you like to live in Canada? Why/Why not?"
- Hilfreiche Redewendungen findest du auf S. 61/62.

Zur **Vorbereitung** auf diesen Prüfungsteil kannst du die folgenden Aufgaben jeweils zweimal verwenden. Da es insgesamt sechs Stichwörter in der Mindmap zur Auswahl gibt, kannst du immer je zwei Sets mit jeweils drei Punkten zusammenstellen und einen kurzen Vortrag vorbereiten, z. B. zum Thema „Canada": Set 1 (*languages, native tribes, cities*), Set 2 (*landscape, tourist attractions, animals*). Es bietet sich auch an, dass du dir selbst ein Thema überlegst und dazu eine Mindmap anfertigst. Übe die Prüfungssituation, indem du dich zu den Stichwörtern äußerst. Stoppe die Zeit, sodass du ein Gefühl entwickelst, wie „lange" es dauert, 2 Minuten zu reden. Du kannst deinen Vortrag auch aufzeichnen und ihn anschließend beurteilen.

5. Look at the mindmap about **Canada**. You have 1 ½ minutes to choose **3 aspects** and prepare what you will say about them. Then start with your 2-minute talk.

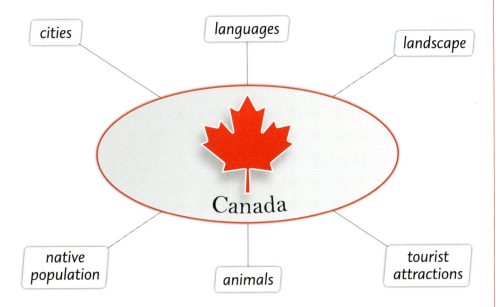

Kompetenzbereich: Sprechen

6. Take a look at the mindmap about **holidays**. You have 1 ½ minutes to choose **3 aspects** and to prepare what you will say about them. Then start with your 2-minute talk.

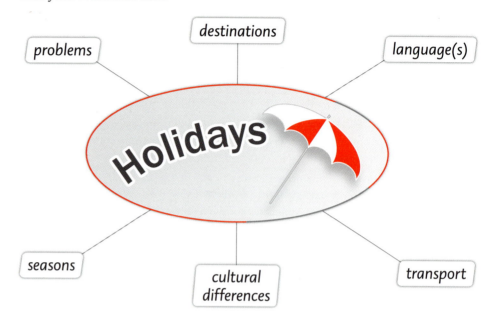

Sprachmittlung

Zunächst wird dir auf Englisch kurz eine Situation vorgestellt. Du erhältst dabei Informationen zum Ort, über die am Gespräch beteiligten Personen, sowie zum Anlass des Gesprächs. Anschließend nehmen die Prüfer/innen und du ihre Rollen ein. Eine prüfende Lehrkraft wird dabei nur Englisch sprechen, die andere nur Deutsch. Deine Aufgabe ist es, ihre Fragen und Aussagen jeweils in die andere Sprache zu übersetzen. Du erhältst keine schriftliche Vorlage des Gesprächs, sondern musst die Inhalte direkt den Aussagen der Prüfenden entnehmen. In der Regel wird dabei satzweise vorgegangen, d. h., der Prüfer trägt einen Satz vor, du übersetzt ihn, anschließend sagt die Lehrkraft den nächsten Satz, usw. Beachte dabei folgende Punkte:

- Übersetze zügig und vermeide lange Pausen, da die Aufgabe nach 5 Minuten beendet wird.
- Du darfst alles direkt übersetzen. Eine Übertragung in die 3. Person wird nicht erwartet, obwohl eine Sprachmittlungssituation vorgegeben wird.
  Beispiel: „Ich möchte eine Packung Schmerztabletten."
  → "I'd like a pack of painkillers, please."; 3. Person: z. B. "The lady would like …"
- Übersetze aber nicht zwangsläufig Wort für Wort, sondern übertrage die Aussagen sinngemäß so, wie es im Englischen oder Deutschen üblich ist.
  Beispiel: "Here you are." → „Bitte schön."
- Umschreibe Wörter, die du nicht kennst, oder ersetze diese durch ein ähnliches Wort.
  Beispiel: „Meine Schuhe sind wirklich bequem."
  → "My shoes fit really well/are really comfortable."
- Keinesfalls solltest du nichts sagen, wenn du etwas nicht übersetzen kannst. Versuche stattdessen, das Gespräch fortzusetzen. Ist die Vorgabe zum Verständnis nicht unbedingt nötig, kannst du sie notfalls überspringen:
  Beispiel: Beim Einkaufen: „Nein, danke. Das ist mir zu teuer. Auf Wiedersehen."
  "No thanks. (…). Goodbye."
- Manchmal kannst du auch die Körpersprache einsetzen, um einen Gegenstand/Sachverhalt zu beschreiben und beim Arzt z. B. auf die Wunde zeigen.

Kompetenzbereich: Sprechen

7. You are in a pharmacy in Wales. Your grandmother needs help from an assistant, but her English isn't good enough. The pharmacist doesn't speak any German. Translate what they say.

   a) **Pharmacist:** Good morning. What can I do for you?

   b) **Großmutter:** Also ich habe ein Problem mit meinem Fuß. Er tut so weh.

   c) **Pharmacist:** Where does it hurt exactly? Could you show me, please?

   d) **Großmutter:** Hier unten. Die Haut ist auch schon rot.

   e) **Pharmacist:** Have you had this problem before?

   f) **Großmutter:** Ich glaube nicht. Es ist neu.

   g) **Pharmacist:** What about your shoes? Is your shoe scratching or rubbing against your skin?

   h) **Großmutter:** Nein. Meine Schuhe sind wirklich bequem.

   i) **Pharmacist:** Well, I think you should see a doctor. There is a very good one next door. Why don't you go there?

   j) **Großmutter:** Das ist eine gute Idee. Das mache ich. Vielen Dank.

   k) **Pharmacist:** Get well soon and goodbye!

© racorn. 123rf.com

Kompetenzbereich: Sprechen

8. You're at a hotel in New York. A German tourist has just arrived and needs help. The tourist doesn't speak English and the receptionist, Mr. Walker, doesn't speak any German. Translate what they say.

a) **Receptionist:** Good afternoon. What can I do for you?

_____

_____

© jordache. Shutterstock

b) **Tourist:** Schmidt, guten Tag. Ich habe eine Reservierung.

_____

c) **Receptionist:** Mr. Schmidt. Your reservation is from 15th to 18th August. Could I have your passport and your credit card, please?

_____

d) **Tourist:** Hier, bitte. Können Sie mich morgen um 6 Uhr wecken?

_____

e) **Receptionist:** Sure! Here's your key. Your room is number 223. Breakfast is served from 6 to 10 a.m. The breakfast room is on the first floor.

_____

f) **Tourist:** Habe ich von meinem Zimmer aus einen schönen Ausblick über die Stadt oder kann ich die Freiheitsstatue sehen?

_____

g) **Receptionist:** Sorry, your room is on the second floor. So there really isn't much of a view, but I think you'll still like your room because it is pretty quiet. You know, quiet rooms are not so typical for New York.

_____

h) **Tourist:** Kein Problem. Kann ich im Hotel Tickets für das Musical "Lion King" kaufen?

_____

i) **Receptionist:** I'm sorry we don't sell theatre tickets. You can buy them at the theatres on Broadway or at the ticket office on Times Square.

_____

j) **Tourist:** Danke. Auf Wiedersehen.

_____

Kompetenzbereich: Sprechen | 89

9. You are at a souvenir shop in London. A German tourist needs help because her English isn't good enough. Mrs Jones, the shop assistant, doesn't speak any German. Translate what they say.

   a) **Assistant:** Hello, can I help you?

   b) **Tourist:** Ja, bitte. Ich hätte gerne dieses blaue T-Shirt in L.

   c) **Assistant:** Here you are.

   d) **Tourist:** Wo kann ich es anprobieren?

   e) **Assistant:** The changing rooms are over there.

   f) **Tourist:** Dieses T-Shirt ist zu groß. Kann ich ein kleineres haben?

   g) **Tourist:** *(Nach dem Anprobieren).* Jetzt passt es. Wie viel kostet es?

   h) **Assistant:** It's £20. Would you like anything else?

   i) **Tourist:** Ich nehme auch diese beiden Postkarten. Verkaufen Sie auch Briefmarken?

   j) **Assistant:** No, I'm sorry. You have to buy them at the post office.

   k) **Tourist:** Schade. Trotzdem danke und auf Wiedersehen.

© Naki Kouyioumtzis. Pearson Education Ltd

TIPP

Reacting to prompts **(Gesprächsführung nach Vorgaben)**

Du erhältst ein Kärtchen, auf dem nicht nur die Situation, sondern auch einige Gesprächsvorgaben bzw. Aufforderungen *(prompts)* in Form von Stichpunkten aufgelistet sind.

Deine Aufgabe ist es nun, entweder alleine einen kurzen Vortrag zu halten oder mit dem Prüfer/der Prüferin ein Gespräch zu führen, in das du die Vorgaben einbaust.

• Verwende alle Vorgaben in deinem Vortrag/dem Gespräch.
• Sprich deutlich in ganzen Sätzen.
• Bringe deine eigenen Ideen in das Gespräch ein.
• Wecke das Interesse deines Gegenübers, indem du Fragen an ihn/sie stellst.
• Formuliere ganze, verständliche Sätze.
• Verwende Redewendungen und achte auf die Aussprache und Grammatik.

10. Telling about a trip

Your friend went on a holiday to England, where he/she and his/her parents went on a bike tour. Tell us about the trip!

▶ last August

▶ 2 weeks

▶ they rented[1] bikes in Bristol

▶ no camping because too cold

▶ only two days of sun, a lot of rain

▶ bike was stolen at train station

▶ happy when holiday was over

1 *to rent (mieten)*

11. At the cinema

Rollenkarte A (pupil)

You are on a trip through Great Britain and want to go to a cinema. You go to the ticket office to buy tickets for yourself and two of your friends.

Here are some prompts you can use:

▶ tickets for "Star Wars" available[1]?

▶ 3

▶ front rows for £ 4 per ticket

▶ time film starts?

▶ where to buy popcorn, coke?

▶ no poster

1 *available (erhältlich)*

Kompetenzbereich: Sprechen | 91

Rollenkarte B (teacher)

You sell tickets at the cinema. You are talking to the customer.

Here are some prompts you can use:

- ▶ hello/help?
- ▶ how many?
- ▶ £6 back row, £4 front row
- ▶ price/anything else?
- ▶ 7 p.m.
- ▶ bar/film poster?

12. The concert

Rollenkarte A

At a concert of your favourite band in Munich, you are standing next to a group of young people who are about your age and speak English. In one of the breaks between the songs you ask one of the boys where they come from. Ask the questions. Here are some prompts you can use:

- ▶ where from?
- ▶ on holiday?
- ▶ like the music?
- ▶ getting a drink – want some?
- ▶ sure, get it
- ▶ my name; be right back

Rollenkarte B

At a concert of your favourite band in Munich, you are standing next to another fan who is about your age and speaks English. In one of the breaks between the songs, he/she asks you where you come from. Answer his/her questions. Here are some prompts you can use.

- ▶ group is from Manchester
- ▶ student exchange[1] with German school
- ▶ great!
- ▶ coke
- ▶ what's your name? / Dylan

1 *student exchange (Schüleraustausch)*

▶ **Kurzgrammatik**

Bildnachweis: © Africa Studio. Shutterstock

Kurzgrammatik

Damit du wichtige Grammatikbereiche noch einmal nachschlagen oder wiederholen kannst, findest du hier die wichtigsten Grammatikregeln mit kurzen Beispielsätzen. Lies die Regeln genau durch und sieh dir die Sätze an. Überlege dir zu jedem Satz ein eigenes Beispiel. Präge dir zu den Regeln jeweils einen Beispielsatz ein. Wenn du eine Regel mit einem bestimmten Beispiel verknüpfen kannst, fällt es dir leichter, dir die Regel zu merken. Auf jeden Fall aber gilt: am Lernen der Regeln (und der Beispiele) führt kein Weg vorbei.

1 Adverbien – *adverbs*

Bildung
Adjektiv + *-ly*

Ausnahmen:
- *-y* am Wortende wird zu *-i*.

- auf einen Konsonanten folgendes *-le* wird zu *-ly*.

- auf einen Konsonanten folgendes *-ic* wird zu *-ically*.
  Ausnahme:

Beachte:
- In einigen Fällen haben Adjektiv und Adverb dieselbe Form.
- Unregelmäßig gebildet wird:
- Endet das Adjektiv auf *-ly*, so kannst du kein Adverb bilden und verwendest deshalb: *in a* + Adjektiv + *manner*

glad	→	gladly
easy	→	easily
funny	→	funnily
simple	→	simply
horrible	→	horribly
probable	→	probably
fantastic	→	fantastically
public	→	publicly

daily, early, fast, hard, long, low, weekly, yearly

good	→	well
friendly	→	in a friendly manner

Verwendung
Adverbien bestimmen
- Verben,

- Adjektive oder

- andere Adverbien näher.

She <u>easily found</u> her way back home.
Sie <u>fand mühelos</u> ihren Weg nach Hause.

This band is <u>extremely famous</u>.
Diese Band ist <u>äußerst berühmt</u>.

He walks <u>very quickly</u>.
Er geht <u>sehr schnell</u>.

2 Bedingungssätze – *if-clauses*

Ein Bedingungssatz besteht aus zwei Teilen: Nebensatz (*if*-Satz) + Hauptsatz.
Im **if-Satz** steht die **Bedingung**, unter der die im **Hauptsatz** genannte **Folge** eintritt.

Bedingungssatz Typ I

Bildung

- *if*-Satz (Bedingung): Gegenwart (*simple present*)

- Hauptsatz (Folge): Zukunft mit *will* (*will-future*)

Der *if*-Satz kann auch nach dem Hauptsatz stehen:

- Hauptsatz: *will-future*

- *if*-Satz: *simple present*

Im Hauptsatz kann statt „*will-future*" auch

- *can* + Grundform des Verbs oder

- *must* + Grundform des Verbs stehen.

If you <u>read</u> this book,
Wenn du dieses Buch liest,

you <u>will learn</u> a lot about Scotland.
erfährst du eine Menge über Schottland.

You <u>will learn</u> a lot about Scotland
Du erfährst eine Menge über Schottland,

if you <u>read</u> this book.
wenn du dieses Buch liest.

If you go to London, you <u>can see</u> Sandy.
Wenn du nach London fährst, kannst du Sandy treffen.

If you go to London, you <u>must visit</u> Big Ben.
Wenn du nach London fährst, musst du dir Big Ben ansehen.

Verwendung

Bedingungssätze vom Typ I verwendet man, wenn die **Bedingung erfüllbar** ist. Man gibt an, was unter bestimmten Bedingungen **geschieht**, **geschehen kann** oder was **geschehen sollte**.

If it's hot, we will go to the beach.
Wenn es heiß ist, gehen wir an den Strand.

If it's hot, we can go to the beach.
Wenn es heiß ist, können wir an den Strand gehen.

If it's hot, we must go to the beach.
Wenn es heiß ist, müssen wir an den Strand gehen.

Bedingungssatz Typ II

Bildung

- *if*-Satz (Bedingung): 1. Vergangenheit (*simple past*)

- Hauptsatz (Folge): Konditional I (*conditional I* = *would* + Grundform des Verbs)

If I <u>went</u> to London,
Wenn ich nach London fahren würde,

I <u>would visit</u> the Tower of London.
würde ich mir den Tower of London ansehen.

Kurzgrammatik ✏ 95

> **Verwendung**
> Typ II verwendet man, wenn die **Bedingung nicht erfüllt**, oder die **Erfüllung der Bedingung eher unwahrscheinlich** ist.

3 Fürwörter – *pronouns*

Besitzanzeigende Fürwörter – *possessive pronouns*

> Besitzanzeigende Fürwörter (*possessive pronouns*) verwendet man, um zu sagen, **was (zu) jemandem gehört**.
> Steht ein besitzanzeigendes Fürwort allein, verwendest du eine andere Form, als wenn es bei einem Substantiv steht:
>
> | mit Substantiv | ohne Substantiv |
> |---|---|
> | *my* | *mine* |
> | *your* | *yours* |
> | *his/her/its* | *his/hers/its* |
> | *our* | *ours* |
> | *your* | *yours* |
> | *their* | *theirs* |

This is my bike. – This is mine.
This is your bike. – This is yours.
This is her bike. – This is hers.
This is our bike. – This is ours.
This is your bike. – This is yours.
This is their bike. – This is theirs.

Rückbezügliche Fürwörter – *reflexive pronouns*

> Die rückbezüglichen Fürwörter (*reflexive pronouns*) **beziehen sich auf das Subjekt** des Satzes **zurück:**
>
> *myself*
> *yourself*
> *himself/herself/itself*
> *ourselves*
> *yourselves*
> *themselves*

I will buy myself a new car.
You will buy yourself a new car.
He will buy himself a new car.
We will buy ourselves a new car.
You will buy yourselves a new car.
They will buy themselves a new car.

each other/one another

> *each other/one another* ist unveränderlich. Es bezieht sich auf **mehrere Personen** und wird mit „sich (gegenseitig), einander" übersetzt.
>
> **Beachte:**
> Einige Verben stehen ohne *each other*, obwohl sie im Deutschen mit „sich" übersetzt werden.

They looked at each other and laughed.
Sie schauten sich (gegenseitig) an und lachten.
oder: Sie schauten einander an und lachten.

to meet	*sich treffen*
to kiss	*sich küssen*
to fall in love	*sich verlieben*

4   Grundform – *infinitive*

Die Grundform mit *to* steht nach

- bestimmten Verben, z. B.:

to *agree*	zustimmen
to *attempt*	versuchen
to *choose*	wählen
to *decide*	entscheiden
to *expect*	erwarten
to *forget*	vergessen
to *hope*	hoffen
to *manage*	schaffen
to *offer*	anbieten
to *plan*	planen
to *promise*	versprechen
to *remember*	an etw. denken
to *seem*	scheinen
to *try*	versuchen
to *want*	wollen

He <u>decided</u> <u>to wait</u>.
Er entschied zu warten.

- bestimmten Substantiven, z. B.:

attempt	Versuch
idea	Idee
plan	Plan
wish	Wunsch

It was her <u>wish</u> <u>to marry</u> in November.
Es war ihr Wunsch, im November zu heiraten.

- bestimmten Adjektiven, z. B.:

certain	sicher
difficult	schwer, schwierig
easy	leicht
hard	schwer, schwierig

It was <u>difficult</u> <u>to follow</u> her.
Es war schwierig, ihr zu folgen.

- den Fragewörtern *what, where, which, who, when, why, how*.

We knew <u>where</u> <u>to find</u> her.
Wir wussten, wo wir sie finden würden.

5   Indirekte Rede – *reported speech*

Die indirekte Rede verwendet man, um **wiederzugeben**, **was eine andere Person gesagt** oder **gefragt hat**.

Bildung

Um die indirekte Rede zu bilden, benötigt man ein **Einleitungsverb**. Häufig verwendete Einleitungsverben sind:

to add, to agree, to answer, to ask, to say, to tell, to think, to want to know

Kurzgrammatik | 97

In der indirekten Rede verändern sich die **Fürwörter**, in bestimmten Fällen auch die **Zeiten** und die **Orts-** und **Zeitangaben**.

Verschiebung der Zeiten:

direkte Rede:	**indirekte Rede:**
Jill <u>says</u>, "I <u>love</u> dancing."	Jill <u>says</u> (that) she <u>loves</u> dancing.
Jill sagt: „Ich tanze sehr gerne."	*Jill sagt, sie tanzt sehr gerne.*
Jill <u>said</u>, "I <u>love</u> dancing."	Jill <u>said</u> (that) she <u>loved</u> dancing.
Jill sagte: „Ich tanze sehr gerne."	*Jill sagte, sie tanze sehr gerne.*

Umformung von Fragesätzen:

Tom: "<u>When did</u> they arrive in England?"	Tom asked <u>when</u> they had arrived in England.
Tom: „Wann sind sie in England ange-kommen?"	*Tom fragte, wann sie in England angekommen seien.*
Tom: "Are they staying at the youth hostel?"	Tom asked <u>if/whether</u> they were staying at the youth hostel.
Tom: „Übernachten sie in der Jugend-herberge?"	*Tom fragte, ob sie in der Jugendherberge über-nachteten.*

Befehle und Aufforderungen:

Tom: "Leave the room."	Tom <u>told</u> <u>me</u> to <u>leave</u> the room.
Tom: „Verlass den Raum."	*Tom forderte mich auf, den Raum zu verlassen.*

6 Modale Hilfsverben – *modal auxiliaries*

Im Englischen gibt es zwei Arten von Hilfsverben: die vollständigen Hilfsverben *to be, to have, to do* und die modalen Hilfsverben *(modal auxiliaries) can, may, must, shall, will.*

Bildung

- Die modalen Hilfsverben haben für alle Personen **nur eine Form**, in der 3. Person Singular also kein *-s*.
- Auf das modale Hilfsverb folgt die **Grundform** des Verbs **ohne *to***.
- **Frage und Verneinung** werden **nicht** mit *do/does/did* **umschrieben**.

I, you, he / she /it, we, you, they } must

You <u>must</u> <u>listen</u> to my new playlist.
Du musst dir meine neue Playlist anhören.

<u>Can</u> I have a cup of coffee, please?
Kann ich bitte eine Tasse Kaffee haben?

Die modalen Hilfsverben können nicht alle Zeiten bilden. Deshalb benötigt man bestimmte **Ersatzformen**.

- **can** (können)
  simple past/conditional I: **could**
  Ersatzform: *to be able to*

- **may** (dürfen)
  conditional: **might**
  Ersatzform: *to be allowed to*

- **must** (müssen)
  Ersatzform: *to have to*

  Beachte:
  must not/mustn't = „nicht dürfen"

  „nicht müssen" = *not + to have to*

- **shall** (sollen)
  conditional I: **should**
  Ersatzform: *to want*

I can sing. / I am able to sing.
Ich kann singen.

You may go home early today. /
You are allowed to go home early today.
Du darfst heute früh nach Hause gehen.

He must be home by ten o'clock. /
He has to be home by ten o'clock.
Er muss um zehn Uhr zu Hause sein.

You must not eat all the cake.
Du darfst nicht den ganzen Kuchen essen.

You don't have to eat all the cake.
Du musst nicht den ganzen Kuchen essen.

Shall I help you? / Do you want me to help you?
Soll ich dir helfen?

7 Konjunktionen – *conjunctions*

Konjunktionen (*conjunctions*) verwendet man, um **zwei Hauptsätze oder Haupt- und Nebensatz miteinander zu verbinden**. Mit Konjunktionen lässt sich ein Text strukturieren, indem man z. B. Ursachen, Folgen oder zeitliche Abfolgen angibt.

after	– nachdem
although	– obwohl
as	– als (zeitlich)
as soon as	– sobald
because	– weil, da
before	– bevor

What will you do after she's gone?
Was wirst du tun, nachdem sie gegangen ist?

Although she was ill, she went to work.
Obwohl sie krank war, ging sie zur Arbeit.

As he came into the room, the telephone rang.
Als er ins Zimmer kam, klingelte das Telefon.

As soon as the band began to play, everybody started dancing.
Sobald die Band zu spielen begann, tanzten alle.

I need a new bike because my old bike has been stolen.
Ich brauche ein neues Rad, weil mein altes Rad gestohlen wurde.

Before he goes to work, he buys a newspaper.
Bevor er zur Arbeit geht, kauft er eine Zeitung.

but	– aber	She likes football <u>but</u> she doesn't like skiing. *Sie mag Fußball, <u>aber</u> sie fährt nicht gerne Ski.*
either … or	– entweder … oder	We can <u>either</u> watch a film <u>or</u> go to a concert. *Wir können uns <u>entweder</u> einen Film ansehen <u>oder</u> in ein Konzert gehen.*
in order to	– um … zu, damit	Peter is in Scotland <u>in order to</u> visit his friend Malcolm. *Peter ist in Schottland, <u>um</u> seinen Freund Malcolm <u>zu</u> besuchen.*
neither … nor	– weder … noch	We can <u>neither</u> eat <u>nor</u> sleep outside. It's raining. *Wir können <u>weder</u> draußen essen <u>noch</u> draußen schlafen. Es regnet.*
so that	– sodass	She shut the door <u>so that</u> the dog couldn't go outside. *Sie machte die Tür zu, <u>sodass</u> der Hund nicht hinaus konnte.*
then	– dann	He bought an ice-cream, and <u>then</u> shared it with Sally. *Er kaufte ein Eis, (und) <u>dann</u> teilte er es mit Sally.*
when	– wenn (zeitlich), sobald	Have a break <u>when</u> you've finished painting. *Mache eine Pause, <u>sobald</u> du fertig gestrichen hast.*
while	– während, solange	<u>While</u> we were in London, we had very good weather. *<u>Während</u> wir in London waren, hatten wir sehr gutes Wetter.*

8 Partizipien – *participles*

Partizip Präsens – *present participle*

Bildung Grundform des Verbs + *-ing*	read	→	read<u>ing</u>
Beachte:		
• Stummes *-e* entfällt.	writ<u>e</u>	→	writ<u>ing</u>
• Nach kurzem betonten Vokal wird der Schlusskonsonant verdoppelt.	sto<u>p</u>	→	sto<u>pp</u>ing
• *-ie* wird zu *-y*.	l<u>ie</u>	→	l<u>y</u>ing

Verwendung

Das Partizip Präsens (present participle) verwendet man u. a.

- zur Bildung der Verlaufsform der Gegenwart,

- zur Bildung der Verlaufsform der Vergangenheit.

Peter is reading.
Peter liest (gerade).

Peter was reading when I came into the room.
Peter las (gerade), als ich in den Raum kam.

Partizip Perfekt – *past participle*

Bildung

Grundform des Verbs + -*ed*

Beachte:

- Stummes -*e* entfällt.

- Nach kurzem betonten Vokal wird der Schlusskonsonant verdoppelt.

- -*y* wird zu -*ie*.

- Unregelmäßige Verben: siehe die Liste in deinem Schulbuch. Die *past-participle*-Formen einiger wichtiger unregelmäßiger Verben sind hier angegeben.

talk	→	talked
live	→	lived
stop	→	stopped
cry	→	cried
be	→	been
have	→	had
give	→	given
go	→	gone
take	→	taken
write	→	written

Verwendung

Das Partizip Perfekt (past participle) verwendet man u. a.

- zur Bildung der zweiten Vergangenheit (present perfect),

- zur Bildung der Vorvergangenheit (past perfect),

- zur Bildung des Passivs.

He has talked to his father.
Er hat mit seinem Vater gesprochen.

Before they went biking in France they had bought new bicycles.
Bevor sie nach Frankreich zum Radfahren gingen, hatten sie neue Fahrräder gekauft.

The fish was eaten by the cat.
Der Fisch wurde von der Katze gefressen.

Kurzgrammatik | **101**

9 Passiv – *passive voice*

Bildung
Form von *to be* + Partizip Perfekt

The picture <u>is made</u> by Peter.
Das Bild wird von Peter gemalt.

Tower Bridge <u>was finished</u> in 1894.
Die Tower Bridge wurde 1894 fertiggestellt.

10 Präpositionen – *prepositions*

Präpositionen (*prepositions*) werden auch als Verhältniswörter bezeichnet. Sie drücken **räumliche, zeitliche oder andere Arten von Beziehungen** aus.

The ball is <u>under</u> the table.
Der Ball ist unter dem Tisch.

He arrived <u>after</u> six o'clock.
Er kam nach sechs Uhr.

I knew it <u>from</u> the start.
Ich wusste es von Anfang an.

Die wichtigsten Präpositionen mit Beispielen für ihre Verwendung:

- at
  Ortsangabe: *at home*

I'm <u>at home</u> at the moment.
Ich bin zurzeit zu Hause.

  Zeitangabe: *at three o'clock*

He arrived <u>at</u> three o'clock.
Er kam um drei Uhr an.

- by
  Angabe des Mittels: *to go by bike*

She went to work <u>by bike</u>.
Sie fuhr mit dem Rad zur Arbeit.

  Angabe der Ursache: *by mistake*

He did it <u>by mistake</u>.
Er hat es aus Versehen getan.

  Zeitangabe: *by tomorrow*

You will get your book back <u>by tomorrow</u>.
Du bekommst dein Buch bis morgen zurück.

- for
  Zeitdauer: *for hours*

We waited for the bus <u>for hours</u>.
Wir haben stundenlang auf den Bus gewartet.

- from
  Ortsangabe: from Dublin

Ian is <u>from Dublin</u>.
Ian kommt aus Dublin.

  Zeitangabe: from nine to five

We work from nine to five.
Wir arbeiten von neun bis fünf Uhr.

- in
  Ortsangabe: in England

<u>In England</u>, they drive on the left.
In England herrscht Linksverkehr.

  Zeitangabe: in the morning

They woke up early <u>in the morning</u>.
Sie wachten am frühen Morgen auf.

Kurzgrammatik

- *of*
  Ortsangabe: *north of the city*

  The village lies <u>north of the city</u>.
  Das Dorf liegt nördlich der Stadt.

- *on*
  Ortsangabe: *on the left, on the floor*

  <u>On the left</u> you see the Empire State Building.
  Links sehen Sie das Empire State Building.

  Zeitangabe: *on Monday*

  <u>On Monday</u> she will buy the tickets.
  (Am) Montag kauft sie die Karten.

- *to*
  Richtungsangabe: *to turn to the left*

  Please <u>turn to the left</u>.
  Bitte wenden Sie sich nach links.

  Angabe des Ziels: *to London*

  He goes <u>to London</u> every year.
  Er fährt jedes Jahr nach London.

Präpositionen kommen häufig in
Orts- und Richtungsangaben vor:

- *behind*

  The ball is <u>behind</u> the chair.

- *in front of*

  The apple is <u>in front of</u> the bottle.

- *next to*

  Kim is <u>next to</u> Colin.

- *near*

  Jenny is <u>near</u> the shop.

- *outside*

  My car is <u>outside</u> my house.

- *inside*

  Paula is <u>inside</u> the bank.

- *under*

  The letter is <u>under</u> the book.

- *on the left*

  My house is <u>on the left</u>.

- *on the right*

  The door is <u>on the right</u>.

- *in the middle (of)*

  My coat is <u>in the middle</u>.
  The bookshop is <u>in the middle of</u> the town.

- *at*

  He is waiting <u>at</u> the bus stop.

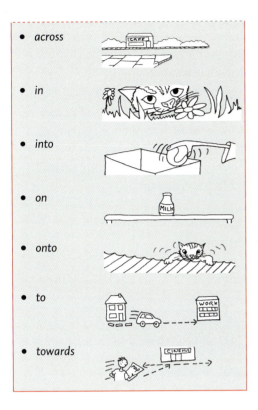

- *across* — The café is across the street.
She walks across the road.
- *in* — The cat is in the garden.
- *into* — Susan is putting the ball into the box.
- *on* — The milk is on the table.
- *onto* — The cat is climbing onto the garage roof.
- *to* — She drives to work.
- *towards* — Max is walking towards the cinema.

11 Relativsätze – *relative clauses*

Ein Relativsatz bezieht sich auf eine Person oder Sache des Hauptsatzes und beschreibt diese näher:

The boy who looks like Jane is her brother.
Der Junge, der Jane ähnlich sieht, ist ihr Bruder.

- Hauptsatz: The boy is her brother
- Relativsatz: who looks like Jane

Bildung

Haupt- und Nebensatz werden durch das Relativpronomen (*who, which, that*) verbunden.

- **who** bezieht sich auf **Personen**.

  Peter, who lives in London, likes travelling.
  Peter, der in London lebt, reist gerne.

- **which** bezieht sich auf **Sachen**.

  The film "Dark Moon", which we saw yesterday, was far too long.
  Der Film „Dark Moon", den wir gestern sahen, war viel zu lang.

- **that** kann sich auf Personen oder Sachen beziehen, ist aber eher umgangssprachlich.

  The film that we saw last week was better.
  Der Film, den wir letzte Woche gesehen haben, war besser.

Verwendung

Mithilfe von Relativsätzen kannst du **zwei Sätze miteinander verbinden**, wenn sie dasselbe Subjekt haben.	London is England's biggest city. London has about 8 million inhabitants. *London ist die größte Stadt Englands. London hat etwa 8 Millionen Einwohner.* London, which is England's biggest city, has about 8 million inhabitants. *London, die größte Stadt Englands, hat etwa 8 Millionen Einwohner.*

12 Steigerung und Vergleich – *comparisons*

Steigerung des Adjektivs – *comparison of adjectives*

Bildung

Man unterscheidet:

- Grundform

  Peter is young.

- 1. Steigerungsform

  Jane is younger.

- 2. Steigerungsform

  Paul is the youngest.

Steigerung auf -er, -est

- einsilbige Adjektive

  old, older, oldest
  alt, älter, am ältesten

- zweisilbige Adjektive, die auf -er, -le, -ow oder -y enden

  clever, cleverer, cleverest
  klug, klüger, am klügsten

  simple, simpler, simplest
  einfach, einfacher, am einfachsten

  narrow, narrower, narrowest
  eng, enger, am engsten

  funny, funnier, funniest
  lustig, lustiger, am lustigsten

Beachte:

- Stummes -e am Wortende entfällt.

  simple, simpler, simplest

- Nach einem Konsonanten wird -y am Wortende zu -i-.

  funny, funnier, funniest

- Nach kurzem Vokal wird ein Konsonant am Wortende verdoppelt.

  fit, fitter, fittest

Steigerung mit *more ..., most ...*

- zweisilbige Adjektive, die nicht auf -er, -le, -ow oder -y enden

  useful, more useful, most useful
  nützlich, nützlicher, am nützlichsten

- Adjektive mit drei und mehr Silben

  difficult, more difficult, most difficult
  schwierig, schwieriger, am schwierigsten

Kurzgrammatik | 105

Unregelmäßige Steigerung

Die unregelmäßig gesteigerten Adjektive solltest du lernen. Einige wichtige Adjektive sind hier angegeben.

good, better, best
gut, besser, am besten

bad, worse, worst
schlecht, schlechter, am schlechtesten

many, more, most
viele, mehr, am meisten

much, more, most
viel, mehr, am meisten

little, less, least
wenig, weniger, am wenigsten

Vergleich – *sentences with comparisons*

Bildung

- Wenn du sagen möchtest, dass **zwei Sachen gleich** sind:
  as + Grundform des Adjektivs + *as*

  Anne is <u>as</u> <u>tall</u> <u>as</u> John.
  Anne ist genauso groß wie John.

- Wenn du sagen möchtest, dass **zwei Sachen ungleich** sind:
  not as + Grundform des Adjektivs + *as*

  John is <u>not as</u> <u>tall</u> <u>as</u> Steve.
  John ist nicht so groß wie Steve.

- Wenn du sagen möchtest, dass **zwei Sachen verschieden** gut/schlecht/ schön … sind:
  1. Steigerungsform des Adjektivs + *than*

  Steve is <u>taller</u> <u>than</u> Anne.
  Steve ist größer als Anne.

Steigerung des Adverbs – *comparison of adverbs of manner*

Adverbien können wie Adjektive auch gesteigert werden.

- Adverbien auf *-ly* werden mit **more, most** bzw. mit **less, least** gesteigert.

  She talks <u>more</u> <u>quickly</u> than John.
  Sie spricht schneller als John.

- Adverbien, die dieselbe Form wie das Adjektiv haben, werden mit **-er, -est** gesteigert.

  fast   –   fast<u>er</u>   –   fast<u>est</u>
  early   –   earl<u>ier</u>   –   earl<u>iest</u>

- Folgende Adverbien haben unregelmäßige Steigerungsformen:

  well   –   better   –   best
  badly   –   worse   –   worst

13 Wortstellung – *word order*

Im englischen Aussagesatz gilt die Wortstellung Subjekt – Prädikat – Objekt (*subject – verb – object*):

- Das Subjekt gibt an, wer oder was etwas tut.

- Das Prädikat gibt an, was getan wird.

- Das Objekt gibt an, worauf/auf wen sich die Tätigkeit bezieht.

Beachte:
- Orts- und Zeitangaben stehen meist am Satzende.

- Ortsangaben stehen vor Zeitangaben.

The cat catches a mouse.

The cat
Die Katze

catches
fängt

a mouse.
eine Maus.

We will buy a new car tomorrow.
Morgen werden wir ein neues Auto kaufen.

Peter lives in New York.
Peter wohnt in New York.

He moved to New York in June.
Er ist im Juni nach New York gezogen.

14 Zeiten – *tenses*

Gegenwart – *simple present*

Bildung
Grundform des Verbs, Ausnahme 3. Person Einzahl: Grundform des Verbs + -s

Beachte:
- Bei Verben, die auf -s, -sh, -ch, -x enden, wird -es angefügt.

- Bei Verben, die auf Konsonant + -y enden, wird -es angefügt; -y wird zu -i-.

Bildung von Fragen im *simple present*
Umschreibung mit Fragewort + *do/does* + Grundform des Verbs

stand – he/she/it stands

kiss – he/she/it kisses
rush – he/she/it rushes
teach – he/she/it teaches
fix – he/she/it fixes
carry – he/she/it carries

Where does he live?
Wo lebt er?

Kurzgrammatik ✐ 107

Beachte:
Die Umschreibung wird nicht verwendet,
- wenn nach dem Subjekt gefragt wird
  (mit *who, what, which*).

Who lives next door?
Wer wohnt nebenan?

What happens next?
Was passiert als Nächstes?

Which tree has more leaves?
Welcher Baum hat mehr Blätter?

- wenn die Frage mit *is/are* gebildet wird.

Are you happy?
Bist du glücklich?

Bildung der Verneinung im *simple present*
Umschreibung mit *don't/doesn't* + Grundform des Verbs

He doesn't like football.
Er mag Fußball nicht.

Verwendung
Das *simple present* beschreibt
- Tätigkeiten, die man gewohnheitsmäßig
  oder häufig ausführt,

Every morning John buys a newspaper.
Jeden Morgen kauft sich John eine Zeitung.

- allgemeingültige Aussagen.

London is a big city.
London ist eine große Stadt.

Signalwörter: *always, every morning, every afternoon, every day, often, never*

Verlaufsform der Gegenwart – *present progressive*

Bildung
am/is/are + Verb in der *-ing*-Form (Partizip
Präsens)

read → am/is/are reading

Bildung von Fragen im *present progressive*
am/is/are + Subjekt + Verb in der *-ing*-Form

Is Peter reading?
Liest Peter gerade?

Bildung der Verneinung im *present progressive*
am not/isn't/aren't + Verb in der *-ing*-Form

Peter isn't reading.
Peter liest gerade nicht.

Verwendung
Mit dem *present progressive* drückt man aus,
- dass etwas **gerade passiert** und **noch
  nicht abgeschlossen** ist.
  Signalwörter: *at the moment, now*

At the moment, Peter is drinking a cup of tea.
Im Augenblick trinkt Peter eine Tasse Tee.
*[Er hat damit angefangen und noch nicht
aufgehört.]*

- dass es um eine **zukünftige**, **bereits
  festgelegte Handlung** geht.

We are seeing the match on Sunday.
Am Sonntag sehen wir uns das Spiel an.

1. Vergangenheit – *simple past*

Bildung

Regelmäßige Verben: Grundform des Verbs + -ed

walk	→	walk**ed**

Beachte:

- Stummes -*e* entfällt.
- Bei Verben, die auf Konsonant + -*y* enden, wird -*y* zu -*i*-.
- Nach kurzem betonten Vokal wird der Schlusskonsonant verdoppelt.

hop**e**	→	hop**ed**
car**ry**	→	car**ried**
st**op**	→	st**opped**

Unregelmäßige Verben: siehe die Liste in deinem Schulbuch. Die *simple-past*-Formen einiger wichtiger unregelmäßiger Verben sind hier angegeben.

be	→	was
have	→	had
give	→	gave
go	→	went
meet	→	met
say	→	said
see	→	saw
take	→	took
write	→	wrote

Bildung von Fragen im *simple past*

Umschreibung mit
Fragewort + *did* + Grundform des Verbs

<u>Why</u> <u>did</u> he <u>look</u> out of the window?
Warum sah er aus dem Fenster?

Beachte:

Die Umschreibung wird nicht verwendet,

- wenn nach dem Subjekt gefragt wird (mit *who, what, which*).

<u>Who</u> <u>paid</u> the bill?
Wer zahlte die Rechnung?

<u>What</u> <u>happened</u> to your friend?
Was ist mit deinem Freund passiert?

<u>Which</u> boy <u>cooked</u> the meal?
Welcher Junge hat das Essen gekocht?

- wenn die Frage mit *were* gebildet wird.

<u>Were</u> you happy?
Warst du glücklich?

Bildung der Verneinung im *simple past*

Umschreibung mit *didn't* + Grundform des Verbs

Why <u>didn't</u> you <u>call</u> me?
Warum hast du mich nicht angerufen?

Verwendung

Das *simple past* beschreibt Handlungen und Ereignisse, die **in der Vergangenheit geschehen** und **bereits abgeschlossen** sind.

Signalwörter: z. B. *yesterday, last week, last year, five years ago, in 1999*

Last week he <u>helped</u> me with my homework.
Letzte Woche half er mir bei meinen Hausaufgaben. [Das Helfen fand in der letzten Woche statt, ist also bereits abgeschlossen.]

Verlaufsform der 1. Vergangenheit – *past progressive*

Bildung:
was/were + Verb in der *-ing*-Form

watch → *was/were* watching

Verwendung
Das *past progressive* verwendet man, wenn zu einem bestimmten Zeitpunkt in der Vergangenheit eine Handlung abläuft, v. a. dann, wenn diese unterbrochen wird.

Yesterday at 11 o'clock I was still sleeping.
Gestern um 11 Uhr habe ich noch geschlafen.

I was reading a book when he came in.
Ich las (gerade) ein Buch, als er herein kam.

2. Vergangenheit – *present perfect simple*

Bildung
have/has + Partizip Perfekt des Verbs

write → has/have written

Verwendung
Das *present perfect simple* verwendet man, wenn

- ein Vorgang in der Vergangenheit begonnen hat und noch andauert,

He has lived in London since 2002.
Er lebt seit 2002 in London.
[Er lebt jetzt immer noch in London.]

- das Ergebnis einer vergangenen Handlung **Auswirkungen auf die Gegenwart** hat.

I have finished my work.
Ich bin mit meiner Arbeit fertig.

Beachte:
have/has können zu *'ve/'s* verkürzt werden.

I've eaten your lunch.
Ich habe dein Mittagessen gegessen.

He's given me his umbrella.
Er hat mir seinen Regenschirm gegeben.

Signalwörter: z. B. *already, ever, just, how long, not … yet, since, for*

Beachte:
Das *present perfect simple* wird oft mit *since* und *for* verwendet (Deutsch: „seit").

- *since* gibt einen **Zeitpunkt** an:

Ron has been married since 1997.
Ron ist seit 1997 verheiratet.

- *for* gibt einen **Zeitraum** an:

Sally has been married for five years.
Sally ist seit fünf Jahren verheiratet.

Verlaufsform der 2. Vergangenheit – *present perfect progressive*

Bildung
have/has + *been* + Partizip Präsens

write → has/have been writing

Kurzgrammatik

Verwendung

Das *present perfect progressive* verwendet man, um die **Dauer einer Handlung** zu **betonen**, die in der Vergangenheit begonnen hat und noch andauert.

She <u>has</u> <u>been</u> <u>sleeping</u> for ten hours.
Sie schläft (schon) seit zehn Stunden.

Zukunft mit *will – will-future*

Bildung

will + Grundform des Verbs

buy   →   <u>will buy</u>

Bildung von Fragen im *will-future*
Fragewort + *will* + Grundform des Verbs

<u>What</u> <u>will</u> you <u>buy</u>?
Was wirst du kaufen?

Bildung der Verneinung im *will-future*
Fragewort + *won't* + Grundform des Verbs

<u>Why</u> <u>won't</u> you <u>come</u> to our party?
Warum kommst du nicht zu unserer Party?

Verwendung

Das *will-future* verwendet man, wenn ein Vorgang **in der Zukunft stattfinden** wird.

Signalwörter: z. B. *tomorrow, next week, next Monday, next year, in three years, soon*

Beachte: Bei geplanten Handlungen verwendet man das *going-to-future*.

It <u>will rain</u> tomorrow.
Morgen wird es regnen.

Zukunft mit *going to – going-to-future*

Bildung

am/is/are + *going to* + Grundform des Verbs

find   →   <u>am/is/are going to find</u>

Verwendung

Das *going-to-future* verwendet man, um auszudrücken, dass eine **Handlung geplant** ist.

I <u>am going to work</u> in England this summer.
Diesen Sommer werde ich in England arbeiten.

Zukunft mit *present progressive*

Verwendung

Mit dem *present progressive* drückt man auch aus, dass es um eine **zukünftige**, **bereits festgelegte Handlung** geht.

We <u>are seeing</u> the match on Sunday.
Am Sonntag sehen wir uns das Spiel an.

▶ **Musteraufgabe und Original-Prüfungsaufgaben**

Bildnachweis: © wavebreakmedia. Shutterstock

| Qualifizierender Abschluss der Mittelschule Bayern
Offizielle Musteraufgabe Englisch | E-1 |

A   Hör- und Hörsehverstehen

Task 1: Mike and Susan are together with their mother on a flight from London to Gibraltar. They want to visit their father who works in Gibraltar.
Listen to the captain of the aircraft speaking to the passengers and answer the questions. Write short answers.
There is an example (0) at the beginning.

5 Punkte

0.   What is the number of the flight?
     BS389

1.   When will the flight arrive?
     _____

2.   What often makes landing at Gibraltar airport difficult?
     _____

3.   Why will today's landing be soft?
     _____

4.   How warm is it in Gibraltar right now?
     _____

5.   On which side can passengers see two famous sights?
     _____

Task 2: After landing at Gibraltar airport, Mike, Susan and their mother are sitting in a taxi and travelling to their hotel.
Listen to their conversation with the taxi driver.
There is one mistake in each sentence. Mark the wrong word.
There is an example (0) at the beginning.

6 Punkte

0.   We've booked a room in the Monkey Rock ~~Hostel~~.

1.   It's only about fifty kilometres away.

2.   The western road is more historical.

3.   The port offers a breathtaking view.

4.   You'll learn something about the environment of Gibraltar.

5.   Since 2014 Sandy Bay has become a private beach again.

6.   A strong storm washed away some of the sand of Sandy Bay.

E-2   Qualifizierender Abschluss der Mittelschule – Englisch Musteraufgabe

7 Punkte

Task 3: Mike, Susan and their mother are on a whale-watching boat now. There is a competition for the passengers. Mike and Susan get a competition form. Listen to the tour guide and the family. While listening, complete the form with information you hear.

There is an example (0) at the beginning.

Whale-Watching Tour

Name: *Susan and Mike*	**Mobile phone:** +4408154711

General information about your tour	
guide	**(0)** *Rufo López*
boat	Queen of Gibraltar
duration	three hours

What have you learnt about …

	dolphins	orcas
length	• up to 2.3 m	• 10 m
weight	• 135 kg	• from 1.6 to 9 tons
speed	• (1) _____ km/h	• 55 km/h
age	• up to 40 years	• (2) up to _____ years
fun facts	• very intelligent • (3) _____ well • produce different (4) _____ • whistle to communicate • have (5) _____ for each other	• also known as killer whales • have a special (6) _____ technique • like tuna • steal fish from the (7) _____

Put the completed form in the box next to the captain's cabin.
With a little bit of luck you can win a snorkelling trip.

Qualifizierender Abschluss der Mittelschule – Englisch Musteraufgabe ✦ E-3

B Sprachgebrauch

1. Read the following text about Gibraltar. Complete it using the correct words. 9 Punkte
   <u>Do not change the text</u>. There is an example (0) at the beginning.

   If you ask people (0) **about** Gibraltar, most of them (1) _____

   tell you about the monkeys. But this bit of land near the southern tip of Spain

   offers (2) _____ more than a big rock with monkeys on it.

   Gibraltar (3) _____ part of the United Kingdom since 1713. It is

   (4) _____ of the UK's 14 overseas territories. Although the land

   itself is not more (5) _____ 6.7 square kilometres in area, it is stra-

   tegically important and the British are determined not to give it back to Spain.

   The territory has (6) _____ own flag and the National Day, Septem-

   ber 10, is a public (7) _____ in Gibraltar. On this day the in-

   habitants all dress (8) _____ red and white, which are their national

   colours. English is the official language of this crown colony but Spanish and

   a local dialect are spoken as well.

   In Gibraltar, unlike most other UK overseas territories, all the cars, buses and

   bikes (9) _____ on the right-hand side of the road.

   All in all, Gibraltar is a melting pot of many cultures.

2. Read the text about a trip to Gibraltar. Fill in the gaps using the words in 9 Punkte
   brackets in the correct form. <u>Do not change the text</u>. There is an example (0)
   at the beginning.

   Last November my family and I wanted to escape the rainy **British** (0 BRIT-

   AIN) winter. So we _____ (1 DECISION) to go on a short trip

   south and booked a _____ (2 FLY) from Manchester to Gibral-

   tar. As we don't like mass _____ (3 TOURIST) we did not visit

   the Monkey Rock, the most famous _____ (4 ATTRACT).

   Instead we went to the Botanic Gardens, a place I would recommend to every-

   one. The gardens and plant houses make it a wonderful _____

   (5 LOCATE) which can be hired for special events like marriages and recep-

   tions. While walking around we were really _____ (6 SURPRISE)

   to see _____ (7 MUSIC) playing in the middle of a beautiful

   arrangement of plants. They were _____ (8 STUDY) practising

   for their next concert in the Botanic Gardens.

   All in all, Gibraltar is not really that different from Britain. In our opinion it is

   quite interesting. We were not _____ (9 BORING) at all. Our

   break was short, but it was very enjoyable.

C Leseverstehen

GIBRALTAR ROCK

A Standing on top of the Rock, you feel as if you are on top of the world. From a height of 426 m you have a truly breathtaking view across the Strait of Gibraltar, where the waters of the Atlantic meet the Mediterranean, to the African coastline about 14.5 kilometres away. If you turn around, you can look west and east along Spain's sunny coastline, and when you look down, you have a bird's eye view of the community far below, with its quays, marinas and bays. Huddled along the narrow strip of land at the foot of the Rock, live the 33,000 people who inhabit this British Overseas Territory at the southern tip of Spain. The famous Rock itself is visible from every point on the territory. It dominates the landscape and is instantly recognisable when you arrive by air or sea.

B As well as being a prominent landmark, the Rock also houses many of Gibraltar's attractions, such as the Moorish Castle, dating back to medieval times, and two networks of tunnels in the rock, more than 50 kilometres long, built by British military forces. There is also a complex of caves, the largest one of which has been converted into a concert hall for about 400 people. There is even a myth that the caves connect to a tunnel under the Strait across to Morocco.

C The Rock is a nature reserve which can be explored on a variety of walking trails. There is also a cable car to take visitors to Upper Rock. The original vegetation on the Rock was forest but it was destroyed over the centuries by tree felling and goat grazing. Now it is mostly covered with grass and small bushes. It is also an important resting place for migrating birds. They stop to rest and feed on their way to Africa and on their way back to Europe in spring.

D Gibraltar's most widely known tourist attraction, the Barbary monkeys, also live on the Rock. Their natural home is in North Africa, but their presence in Gibraltar dates from the early days of British occupation when they probably were imported. The 300 monkeys which now live in five healthy troops on the steep slopes of the Rock are the only wild monkey population in Europe. In 2012, because of rising numbers, there was even talk of sending some one hundred monkeys back to Africa. The wardens of the nature reserve still want visitors to have 'the monkey experience' but experts have warned that too much human interaction is harmful to these wild animals.

E The monkeys are portrayed on Gibraltar's five-pence coin and many legends have grown up around them. One is that they travelled to Gibraltar from their native Africa via an underground tunnel underneath the Strait of Gibraltar. Another legend says that, should the monkeys ever disappear, the British will leave Gibraltar. By the end of the Second World War, the number of monkeys had gone down dramatically due to disease and other natural causes. Fortunately, Sir Winston Churchill, the British Prime Minister at the time, took a personal interest and additional animals were imported from Morocco. In 1954 they were even visited by Queen Elizabeth II while she and Prince Philip were in Gibraltar.

F The Rock's latest attraction, the Skywalk, was opened in March 2018. It is located at 340 metres above sea-level, which is higher up than the highest point of London's tallest skyscraper, The Shard. Through its glass floor, the Skywalk offers a unique view to the bottom of the Rock. It is built on the foundations of a military lookout point and is designed to carry a load equivalent to five Asian elephants, or 340 people, but visitor numbers are limited to 50 at any one time. As a visitor from England said: "Standing on a sheet of glass hundreds of feet up in the air is not everybody's cup of tea, but the views are outstanding."

Qualifizierender Abschluss der Mittelschule – Englisch Musteraufgabe E-5

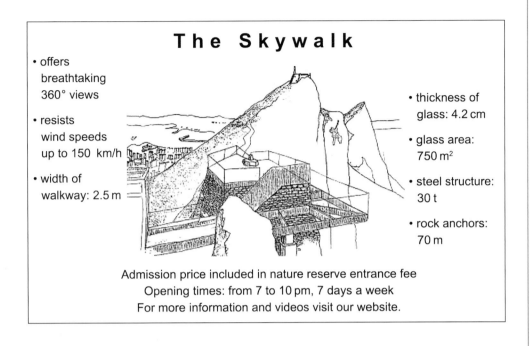

The Skywalk

- offers breathtaking 360° views
- resists wind speeds up to 150 km/h
- width of walkway: 2.5 m
- thickness of glass: 4.2 cm
- glass area: 750 m²
- steel structure: 30 t
- rock anchors: 70 m

Admission price included in nature reserve entrance fee
Opening times: from 7 to 10 pm, 7 days a week
For more information and videos visit our website.

1. Read the text on pages 4 and 5. Match the titles (1–8) to the paragraphs (A–F). Write the correct number in the boxes below. Use each number only once. There are two extra titles. One title (6) is already matched.

    1. At the edge of a continent
    2. A labyrinth below the ground
    3. Climbing on the Rock
    4. Environmental changes on the Rock
    5. A challenging experience
    6. Myths and politics
    7. Growing visitor numbers
    8. Important and popular animals

A	B	C	D	E	F
				6	

    5 Punkte

2. Answer the questions using information from the text on page 4. Short answers are enough.
    There is an example (0) at the beginning.

    0. What is between the Atlantic and the Mediterranean?
    the Strait of Gibraltar

    1. Which construction dates back to the Middle Ages?
    _____

    2. How can you get to the top of the Rock comfortably?
    _____

    6 Punkte

E-6 ✦ Qualifizierender Abschluss der Mittelschule – Englisch Musteraufgabe

3. What kind of animals use the Rock when travelling?

_____

4. What is dangerous for the monkey population?

_____

5. The Skywalk is compared to which building?

_____

6. What weight can the glass floor hold?

_____

4 Punkte

3. Read paragraphs D and E on page 4. Put the events into the order in which they actually happened. Write the numbers 1–6 into the table below. Two events (1 and 4) have already been entered.
Use each number only once. There is one event you do not need.

The monkeys lived only in Africa.	1
Some monkeys were sent on to Spain.	
Today's monkey population is doing fine.	
The number of monkeys grew fast.	
A politician decided to bring more monkeys in.	
The monkeys received royal attention.	4
The monkeys arrived in Gibraltar.	

3 Punkte

4. Four of the following statements (a–i) are <u>true</u> according to the information given in the text on pages 4 and 5. One of the true statements (a) has already been found.
Find the remaining <u>three</u> true statements and write the letters on the lines below.

a   There is a town below the Rock.

b   Gibraltar shares a border with Britain.

c   There is an event location inside the Rock.

d   There is a tunnel between Gibraltar and Africa.

e   The Rock can be reached on foot.

f   The monkeys are shown on a banknote.

g   The Skywalk is only open in the mornings.

h   Entrance to the Skywalk is free.

i   The Skywalk is safe during high winds.

True statements
(0) **a**
(1) _____
(2) _____
(3) _____

Qualifizierender Abschluss der Mittelschule – Englisch Musteraufgabe ✦ E-7

9 Punkte

D Sprachmittlung

THE MONKEYS OF GIBRALTAR

1 Apparently, there has been a population of monkeys on Gibraltar Rock for a very long time. However, the legend that brought the monkeys their widespread popularity actually comes from a later period: the time of the Great Siege between 1779 and 1783. The French and Spanish forces made a combined effort to take control of the
5 Rock from the British. In the course of a surprise attack one evening, the monkeys were disturbed and started to make a lot of noise. This drew the attention of the British, and the French and Spanish attack was unsuccessful. It was this event which started the legend that as long as there are monkeys on the Rock of Gibraltar, the British will keep control of the territory.
10 Visitors who want to get close to the monkeys are advised to stay in the open areas. If you meet the monkeys in narrow spaces, on the staircases in the tunnels, for example, the monkeys might feel cornered and then will react aggressively. In such a situation it is best to go back a little and give the monkeys more space. In the company of the monkeys it is not a good idea to crouch down; this might be seen as an invitation to
15 climb up or jump on your back. A final word of warning: the monkeys are very curious and they like to steal bags or handbags, and especially anything that could contain food. Over the years, people in Gibraltar have learnt how to treat their animal neighbours. A lot of human food is bad for the monkeys' health. If the public feed them it also damages the monkeys' social structures: the monkeys live in a community in which
20 each one has a certain role. This group structure and hierarchy is damaged by human influence. What is more, when tourists feed them, it makes them dependent on humans. For these reasons, it is officially forbidden to feed them. Anyone who is caught feeding them has to pay a very high fine.

As long as visitors take these warnings seriously, there is no reason why they shouldn't
25 enjoy meeting the monkeys. Indeed, no visit to Gibraltar would be really complete without it.

E-8 ✦ Qualifizierender Abschluss der Mittelschule – Englisch Musteraufgabe

In der nächsten Ausgabe eurer Schülerzeitung geht es um das Thema Gibraltar. Du schreibst einen Beitrag über den Affenfelsen. Informationen dazu hast du bereits in einem englischen Text gefunden. Lies den Text auf Seite 7 und stelle für deinen Beitrag wichtige Informationen in einem zusammenhängenden Text <u>auf Deutsch</u> zusammen. Gehe dabei auf die wesentlichen Bereiche ein:

- *„Gibraltar bleibt britisch, so lange es Affen auf dem Felsen gibt."*
  Fasse den Ursprung dieser Legende in drei bis vier Sätzen zusammen.

- Beschreibe kurz das Verhalten der Affen im Kontakt mit Menschen.

- Formuliere <u>zwei</u> Verhaltenstipps für Personen, die den Affenfelsen besuchen.

- Beschreibe <u>zwei</u> Folgen des Kontaktes mit den Menschen für die Affen.

> „Gibraltar bleibt britisch, so lange es Affen auf dem Felsen gibt", sagt eine Legende.

Affe © Christian Wittmann. Shutterstock

Qualifizierender Abschluss der Mittelschule – Englisch Musteraufgabe | E-9

E   Text- und Medienkompetenzen

9 Punkte

A BAD EXPERIENCE

Robin H. (+441764391709)

Monday, June 15

OMG, Kim! You won't believe what happened to me today!   12:31

What happened?   12:31

Remember, I'm in Gibraltar with some friends. So today, right after breakfast, we went to Gibraltar Rock. You know, where the famous monkeys are.   12:32

Yes. And?   12:32

And, when we left the cable car at the middle station, a monkey came, grabbed my backpack and ran away with it.   12:32

OMG. LOL. That is so funny. :-)   12:31

No, it's not. >:-(
My passport, the key to my hotel room and my bank card were in it.   12:33

How awful. Do you have any money with you?   12:33

Not a penny. All my money was in there, too. And it's my favourite backpack.   12:33

Oh no! The black one?   12:33

Yeah, that one … the one with the broken zip. And the silver key ring you gave me was attached to it.   12:34

That's too bad. It was really nice with the silver "R" on it. Did you go and look for it?   12:34

We searched the whole area, but we couldn't find the backpack. I really don't know what to do.   12:34

Maybe you could put up posters or post something on social media.   12:38

Yeah! Thanks, Kim. That's a great idea. I will put up posters all over town and offer a reward.   12:39

Read the text on page 9. Then help Robin find the backpack.
Write a helpful headline and complete the poster.

(1) _____

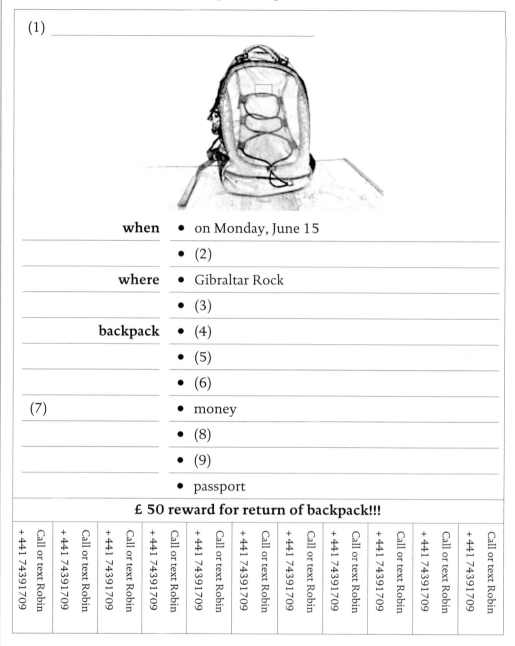

when	•	on Monday, June 15
	•	(2)
where	•	Gibraltar Rock
	•	(3)
backpack	•	(4)
	•	(5)
	•	(6)
(7)	•	money
	•	(8)
	•	(9)
	•	passport

£ 50 reward for return of backpack!!!

Call or text Robin +441 74391709

| Qualifizierender Abschluss der Mittelschule – Englisch Musteraufgabe | E-11 |

F Schreiben

20 Punkte

Wähle eine Aufgabe:

Correspondence: E-mail

oder

Creative Writing: Picture story

E-mail

Du wirst während deines zweiwöchigen Schüleraustausches bei Dani in Marbella, einer Stadt in Spanien, wohnen.

Schreibe Dani eine E-Mail auf Englisch.

- Stell dich kurz vor.
- Erkundige dich nach:
  - Unterbringung, z. B. eigenes Zimmer, Internet
  - Wetteraussichten
  - Schule: Unterrichtszeiten und Regeln
  - Programm: Veranstaltungen und Freizeit
- Äußere folgende Wünsche:
  - Besuch von Gibraltar
  - vegetarisches Essen
- Richte Grüße an Danis Familie aus.

Schreibe eine E-Mail von ungefähr **100 Wörtern** auf ein gesondertes Blatt. Achte auf eine ansprechende äußere Form und eine gut lesbare Handschrift.

Picture story

Schreibe eine Geschichte auf Englisch, in der du alle Bilder berücksichtigst.

Beginne wie folgt:

Happy Ending
Last Monday morning, during the first lesson, ...

Schreibe eine Geschichte von ungefähr **100 Wörtern** auf ein gesondertes Blatt. Achte auf eine ansprechende äußere Form und eine gut lesbare Handschrift.

Qualifizierender Abschluss der Mittelschule Bayern 2014
Englisch

E 2014-1

A Listening Comprehension (No dictionary allowed)

Task 1: Kate and Mike are on holiday in the United States. They are talking to a receptionist at a hotel in Washington DC. Listen and fill in the missing information. There is an example at the beginning (0).

8 Punkte

0. Kate and Mike booked the room **on the internet**.
1. The receptionist wants to see their _____.
2. It's Kate and Mike's _____ visit to Washington DC.
3. They are leaving on _____.
4. They would like a room which is at _____ of the hotel.
5. The Wi-Fi password is _____.
6. They should take a _____ or a bus to get to the White House.
7. The bus stop is _____ the hotel.
8. Breakfast is from _____ till _____.

Task 2: Kate and Mike are doing a tour of the White House. They are listening to an audio guide. Listen and answer the questions. Write short answers. There is an example at the beginning (0).

6 Punkte

0. How long did it take to build the White House?
   8 years

1. How many rooms are there in the White House?
   _____

2. Where are the maps in the Map Room?
   _____

3. Who does the President invite to play basketball at the White House? (<u>one</u> example)
   _____

4. What does Mrs. Obama hope will be a learning experience?
   _____

5. What is in the library except for books?
   _____

6. Where do the First Family and their guests watch films?
   _____

E 2014-2 ✎   Qualifizierender Abschluss der Mittelschule – Englisch 2014

6 Punkte

Task 3: Back at the hotel Kate and Mike are planning their trip to the Grand Canyon. Mike is reading about it on his computer.
Listen and complete the table. Some information is already given.

	Hiking tour	**Helicopter tour**	**Tour from Grand Canyon Airport**
Costs per person?	**No costs**	$ _____	$ _____ online booking
Hours/minutes?	_____	**3 hours**	_____
Problems?	_____ (<u>one</u> example)	_____ (<u>one</u> example)	**no stop in the Canyon**

B Use of English (No dictionary allowed)

6 Punkte

1. Complete the sentences using the correct word from the box. There are some extra words in the box. There is an example at the beginning (0).

   > at – became – become – by – for – from – gets – got – in – of – on
   > really – she – want – wants – where – which – who – will – with
   > worked – working – works – would

   Julia, 17, is one (**0**) **of** the students at her high school (1) _____ has already got a place at college. She really enjoys (2) _____ on the computer and she's very good (3) _____ designing websites. On her last birthday she (4) _____ a new computer from her parents. In her vacation Julia (5) _____ like to do work experience at a software firm in Boston. She has already applied (6) _____ a job at three different companies but she's still waiting to hear from them.

4 Punkte

2. Read the text and complete the sentences. There is an example at the beginning (0).

   Tom is a (**0**) **student** at a high school in Boston. Every morning he checks his (1) **s**_____ to see if he has everything he needs: his books, his calculator and his pencil case. As he is doing a Spanish test today, Tom has to take his (2) **d**_____ to look up the words he doesn't know. He likes biology and English very much, but his favorite (3) **s**_____ is sports. In summer students use the sports fields but in winter they do sport in the (4) **g**_____.

Qualifizierender Abschluss der Mittelschule – Englisch 2014 | ✐ E 2014-3

3. Read the text and fill in the gaps using the words in brackets in the correct | 6 Punkte
   form. There is an example at the beginning (0).

   As everybody (**0** know) **knows**, driving a car is very important in the USA.
   In some states people can get a driving license when they are 16. About two
   weeks ago Steven (**1** begin) _____ learning how to drive.
   The first lesson (**2** not be) _____ easy. He isn't having
   lessons at a driving school because his father (**3** be) _____ his
   instructor. Every Saturday Steven (**4** work) _____ at a local
   supermarket. He (**5** have) _____ the job for over a year
   now. If he saves enough money, he (**6** buy) _____ himself
   a decent second-hand car next year.

4. Complete the interview with the missing questions. There is an example at | 4 Punkte
   the beginning (0).

   Tim: (**0**) **Can you help me, please?** I have to give a talk about American
          schools.

   Jill: Of course, I can help you.

   Tim: (1) _____ some questions?

   Jill: Sure. Just feel free to ask.

   Tim: (2) _____ in the morning?

   Jill: We start at 9. But before that I meet my friends.

   Tim: (3) _____ them?

   Jill: In the school cafeteria. We have breakfast there.

   Tim: (4) _____ your own food?

   Jill: No we don't. We have to buy the food at the cafeteria.

C   Reading Comprehension (Dictionary allowed)

The First Daughters

1 The US president and the First Lady are always in the public eye. Everywhere Barack Obama and his wife Michelle go there are TV cameras, journalists and photographers. (0) _____. But what about their daughters, 13-year-old Sasha and 16-year-old Malia? What is life like for the "First Daughters"?

5 During the last six years Sasha (short for "Natasha") and Malia Obama have traveled all over the world on Air Force One, the US president's airplane. They have met lots of well-known people: kings and queens, political leaders, actors and actresses, sports stars and pop legends. (1) _____. Every week they see pictures of themselves in magazines and newspapers. It is an incredible way of life for the two teen-
10 agers but it is not always easy.

If your dad is the most powerful man in the world, you have to be careful what you do and what you say. (2) _____. "Don't forget," says Michelle Obama. "They're the first
15 kids living in the White House in a time where everybody's got a cell phone and everybody's watching. When they're with their dad while he's making a speech they have to listen and smile." Mrs. Obama goes on: "The last thing
20 you want is yawning."

The President and First Lady are constantly reminding their daughters that they're growing up in a slightly unreal environment at the White House. (3) _____. So when the
25 girls are not with White House staff, their parents expect them to help at home. They have to make their own beds, set the table and take Bo and Sunny, the family dogs, for walks. "We talk a lot about responsibility," says Mrs. Oba-
30 ma. "I tell the girls that they're not going to be in the White House for ever. Not long from now they'll be at college by themselves."

> **Michelle Obama's Rules for Sasha and Malia**
>
> **Technology**
> No TV, no internet and no cell phones during the school week. Only on the weekend.
>
> **Sports**
> The girls have to do two sports: one they choose and one chosen by their mother. "I want them to understand what it feels like to do something you don't like and to improve," Michelle Obama explains.
>
> **Trips**
> When the girls go on trips, they have to write reports about what they saw, both for themselves and their parents.

Although the President and his wife are both very busy, they spend as much time as they can with their children. If possible, all of them sit down to have dinner together
35 at 6.30 pm. (4) _____. Barack Obama likes to know what his daughters are doing in class, how much homework they have and also what they are up to outside school. Like all parents, he is extremely proud of his children. "They're smart, they're funny and they're respectful. I could not have asked for better kids."

So far Barack and Michelle Obama have done everything they can to make sure Sasha
40 and Malia grow up like any other teenager in the US. The girls are allowed to have sleepovers and they can go to the shopping mall or to the movies with their friends. Soon they will also learn how to drive. (5) _____. What about meeting boys? The President smiles, "I've got tough guys with guns looking after my daughters. Any young man who can get past Secret Service deserves a chance!"

adapted from: Jodi Kantor: Obama Girls' Role: Not to Speak, but to Be Spoken Of. In: The New York Times, September 6, 2012. Krissah Thompson: For Sasha and Malia Obama, four more years as the first daughters. In: The Washington Post, November 7, 2012.

| Qualifizierender Abschluss der Mittelschule – Englisch 2014 | E 2014-5 |

1. Find the correct title (A – G) for each paragraph in the text on page 4. There is one extra title. One title is already matched.

5 Punkte

A   Behavior in public

B   Daily chores

C   Famous parents

D   Vacation with the family

E   **Time with the family**

F   Teenage fun

G   Famous teenagers

paragraph 1 (lines 1–4)	
paragraph 2 (lines 5–10)	
paragraph 3 (lines 11–20)	
paragraph 4 (lines 21–32)	
paragraph 5 (lines 33–38)	E
paragraph 6 (lines 39–44)	

2. Five sentences are missing in the text on page 4. Read the sentences (A–G) and match them with the gaps (1–5) in the text. There is one extra sentence. There is an example at the beginning (0).

5 Punkte

A   And then there's dating.

B   During meal times, they have a lot to talk about.

C   **No wonder – the Obamas are stars.**

D   People are looking at you, not just at your dad.

E   That's why Michelle Obama picks a sport for them.

F   They keep telling them that in a "normal" home things are different.

G   They shake their hands and get to talk to them.

(0)	(1)	(2)	(3)	(4)	(5)
C					

3. Answer the questions using information from the text on page 4. Write short answers. There is an example at the beginning (0).

4 Punkte

0. How old are the President's daughters?
   13 and 16

1. What is the President's aircraft called?

   _____

2. When are Sasha and Malia allowed to use the internet?

   _____

3. Which jobs do Sasha and Malia have to do at home? (one example)

   _____

E 2014-6 · Qualifizierender Abschluss der Mittelschule – Englisch 2014

4. Which free time activities can the girls do with other teenagers?
    (<u>one</u> example)

6 Punkte   4. Read the text on page 4 and complete the task below. There is an example at
    the beginning (0).

Which part from the text tells you ...

0. that people are always watching the President and his wife?
    The US President and the First Lady are always in the public eye.

1. that Sasha and Malia know lots of celebrities personally?

2. what Sasha and Malia must do while their dad is speaking in public?

3. that the girls will only live in their present home for a few more years?

4. that Michelle Obama wants to read about the places her girls visited?

5. that Barack Obama has a high opinion of his daughters?

6. that Malia and Sasha are well protected?

Qualifizierender Abschluss der Mittelschule – Englisch 2014 | ✐ E 2014-7

D   Text Production (Dictionary allowed)

20 Punkte

Wähle eine Aufgabe:

I. Correspondence: **E-Mail** or II. Creative Writing: **Picture-Based Story**

I.   **Correspondence:** E-Mail

Du suchst seit längerem einen Ferienjob in den USA. Von der Freundin deiner Tante Emma hast du eine E-Mail mit einem Angebot bekommen, das du annehmen willst.

Beantworte folgende E-Mail von Susan auf Englisch.

Hi,

We heard from Emma that you are looking for a job during your summer holidays. How about coming to San Francisco and helping us?

As Pete and I are both working in July and August, we need somebody to look after our son Justin, 5. He is an energetic, curious boy and always up to new adventures.

From your aunt Emma we've already heard a little bit about you, but we would like to know more:

- Please tell us about your experience of working with children.
- And what about your English?
- When would you be able to come, and how long could you stay?

We would also be happy to answer your questions about Justin, the job, free time, …

We really hope you can come.

Best wishes,

Susan

Schreibe eine E-Mail von ungefähr **12 Sätzen** bzw. etwa **100 Wörtern** auf ein extra Blatt. Denke an eine ansprechende äußere Form.

II. **Creative Writing:** Picture-Based Story
Betrachte die Bilder und schreibe eine Geschichte auf Englisch.
Beginne wie folgt:

The big catch

Last summer Steve and his granddad were at the seaside ...

The next day ...

Schreibe eine Geschichte von ungefähr **12 Sätzen** bzw. etwa **100 Wörtern** auf ein extra Blatt. Denke an eine ansprechende äußere Form.

Qualifizierender Abschluss der Mittelschule Bayern 2015
Englisch

E 2015-1

A Listening Comprehension (No dictionary allowed)

There are four parts to the test. You'll hear each part twice. At the and of each part you'll have some time to complete the tasks.

Task 1: Martin wants to travel to Scotland by coach. He is at a coach station in London talking to the woman at the ticket counter.
Listen and answer the questions. Write short answers. There is an example at the beginning (0).

6 Punkte

0. Where does Martin want to go?
   (to) Aberdeen

1. When does the coach usually leave?

   _____

2. Why is the coach late?

   _____

3. When will the coach leave today?

   _____

4. How many pieces of luggage does Martin have?

   _____

5. How much is Martin's ticket if he leaves on the next coach?

   _____

6. How much can you save if you buy a ticket online?

   _____

Task 2: Two days later Martin is on the coach. He is listening to the coach driver. There is <u>one</u> mistake in each sentence. Listen and write down the correct word(s) on the line. There is an example at the beginning (0).

5 Punkte

0. Good ~~evening~~. I'm John, your driver today.
   morning

1. We're about half an hour late.

   _____

2. We won't be able to make that up by around lunchtime.

   _____

3. The heating's not working properly.

_____

4. There's no on-board service available.

_____

5. There's going to be a change of tyres.

_____

5 Punkte

Task 3: On the coach Martin is talking to an American tourist.
Listen and fill in the missing information. There is an example at the beginning (0).

0. Martin is going to **Aberdeen**.

1. The American tourist is staying with a _____ near Edinburgh.

2. The American thinks the youth hostels in Aberdeen will be _____.

3. Martin would need a _____ for camping.

4. Stonehaven is a _____ close to Aberdeen.

5. In Stonehaven Martin could stay at a _____.

4 Punkte

Task 4: Martin is listening to a guide explaining the Highland Games' competitions. Which of the four pictures shows the competition?
Listen and tick (✓) the correct picture. There is an example at the beginning (0).

0. Bagpiping

☐   ✓   ☐   ☐

1. Weight throw

☐   ☐   ☐   ☐

2. Sheaf toss

☐ ☐ ☐ ☐

3. Tossing the caber

☐ ☐ ☐ ☐

4. Tug of war

☐ ☐ ☐ ☐

B Use of English (No dictionary allowed)

1. Scotland
   Read the text and complete each sentence with <u>one</u> suitable word.
   There is an example at the beginning (0).

   Scotland is (0) **part** of the United Kingdom.
   More (1) _____ five million people live there. Edinburgh, its
   capital, is the second largest (2) _____. Aberdeen is called
   Europe's oil capital (3) _____ Scotland has the largest oil
   reserves in the European Union. Scotland is famous (4) _____
   its lakes and mountains. All year round you (5) _____ find
   lots of tourists travelling the country. So, (6) _____ you
   interested in visiting Scotland?

6 Punkte

E 2015-4 / Qualifizierender Abschluss der Mittelschule – Englisch 2015

6 Punkte

2. The Edinburgh Festival
Read the text and fill in the gaps using the words in brackets in the correct form. There is an example at the beginning (0).

Thousands of (0 tourist) **tourists** go to Edinburgh every year to experience the Festival.

The Edinburgh Festival is one of the (1 big) _____ events in Scotland. People from Scotland and many other (2 country) _____ go there. Last August Tim (3 go) _____ there for the first time. He (4 not stay) _____ long but he enjoyed it. Tim likes (5 get) _____ to know different cultures. That's why he (6 fly) _____ to the USA next year.

8 Punkte

3. An email from Scotland
Read the email. There is <u>one</u> mistake in each line. Circle the letter below the mistake. There is an example at the beginning (0).

Hi Daniel,

0. **Who** <u>are</u> you doing? <u>I'm having</u> a great time <u>in</u> Glasgow!
   (A)   B   C   D

1. <u>On</u> Monday I <u>climbed</u> Ben Nevis, the <u>most high</u> mountain <u>in Great Britain</u>.
   A   B   C   D

2. On the way <u>down</u> I <u>fell</u> and ruined <u>my</u> jeans but I didn't hurt <u>me</u>.
               A   B   C   D

3. <u>The next day</u> I <u>met</u> a man <u>which</u> <u>showed</u> me how to play the bagpipes.
   A   B   C   D

4. <u>The</u> weather <u>has been</u> <u>really</u> good so far: sunny and warm <u>all time</u>.
   A   B   C   D

5. The best thing is: I <u>haven't met</u> <u>some</u> unfriendly <u>people</u>. <u>Everybody</u> is nice.
                        A   B   C   D

6. If they speak <u>slow</u>, I <u>can</u> even understand <u>their</u> Scottish <u>accent</u>.
                  A   B   C   D

7. At the moment I'm <u>at</u> the railway station. <u>I'm waiting</u> <u>of</u> my train <u>to</u>
                      A   B   C   D
   Edinburgh.

8. <u>I'm looking forward</u> <u>to</u> Edinburgh. <u>There are</u> so <u>much</u> things to see
   A   B   C   D
   there!

I'll call you from there.
Love,
Hanna

C Reading Comprehension (Dictionary allowed)

The fastest woman on earth

1 Susie Wolff can drive fast – very fast. Last year the 32-year-old took part in practice sessions at the Formula One Grand Prix in Britain and Germany. This made her the first woman in almost 40 years to drive in an official Formula One event. The last time a woman did so was in 1975 when Lella Lombardi, an Italian driver, raced in
5 South Africa. Susie is much more than just a great driver. She is a role model for women who want to be successful in a profession dominated by men.

Susie Stoddart was born in Scotland in 1982. She began riding a four-wheel bike at the age of two. "I was competitive about everything I did: swimming, skiing, karting. I couldn't have asked for a better start in life – my parents never made me feel I was
10 doing anything unusual for a girl. It wasn't until I was in my teens that I realised there weren't many other women in motorsport," she said in a newspaper interview recently. "Racing's in my blood. My mum met my dad when she went to buy her first motorbike in his shop."

It was not long before Susie won her first races. When she was 14, she was named
15 British Woman Kart Racing Driver of the Year. And it was only one year later that she was first in the 24-hour Middle East Kart Championship. Soon Susie made the step up from kart racing to Formula Three. From there she moved to the DTM, the German Touring Car series, racing for a well-known German car manufacturer.

In 2011 Susie became Susie Wolff when she married Toto Wolff and took his name.
20 Her husband is an ex-racing driver with close links to Formula One. So it was no big surprise that she soon became a development driver for a British Formula One team. Now she is even an official test driver. This year in December, Susie will turn 33. Do the Wolffs plan to have children soon? "I'm in no rush," Susie once told reporters. "But when I have kids, I won't be racing."

25 To drive a Formula One racing car you need great driving skills. But you also need great physical strength. What does that mean for a racing driver? Going round tight corners at high speeds can feel as if 40 kilograms are pressed against your head and neck. This is why many people don't believe women can compete with men in Formula One. For them, motorsport is only for men. If anyone can show them they're
30 wrong, it's Susie Wolff. Susie is careful about what she eats and trains for two hours every day. She is small and light and in Formula One that's an advantage. Susie weighs about 20 kilos less than male drivers, so engineers can add extra equipment to optimize her car.

Wolff has been called the fastest woman on earth so is she scared going at
35 300 kilometres per hour round a racing track? Like all Formula One drivers, she knows about the risks. But as soon as she is in the cockpit she concentrates on the race. "Fear never comes into it," Susie explained in a newspaper interview. "The only fear I've ever experienced is failure." And when she's not in a racing car? Does Susie drive carefully? "When I'm on the motorway, I'm a little bit impatient but never
40 crazy," she admits.

E 2015-6 Qualifizierender Abschluss der Mittelschule – Englisch 2015

5 Punkte

1. Read the text on page 5. Match the correct titles (A–H) to the paragraphs. Write the correct letter in the boxes below. Use the letters only once. There are two extra titles. One title is already matched.

A   An athletic female racer

B   **A great female racing driver**

C   Charity events

D   Childhood and teenage years

E   The road is not a race course

F   Early successes

G   Formula One career and family

H   School and education

paragraph 1 (lines 1–6)	**B**
paragraph 2 (lines 7–13)	
paragraph 3 (lines 14–18)	
paragraph 4 (lines 19–24)	
paragraph 5 (lines 25–33)	
paragraph 6 (lines 34–40)	

5 Punkte

2. Answer the questions using information from the text on page 5. Short answers are possible. There is an example at the beginning (0).

0. Where does Lella Lombardi come from? **Italy**

1. When did Susie find out that racing is unusual for women?

_____

2. How did her parents get to know each other?

_____

3. Who helped her with connections to Formula One?

_____

4. Which parts of the body are especially under pressure during a race?

_____

5. What does she do in order to stay fit?

_____

5 Punkte

3. Read the text on page 5. Which lines tell you the same as the following sentences? Write the number of the line or the lines in the box. There is an example at the beginning (0).

	line or lines
0. For nearly four decades no woman took part in a Formula One race.	**2–3**
1. As a child Susie always wanted to win.	
2. She won an important competition at the age of 15.	
3. Susie is in no hurry to become a mother.	
4. A Formula One driver must be fit and strong.	
5. Susie understands that racing can be dangerous.	

Qualifizierender Abschluss der Mittelschule – Englisch 2015   ✦ E 2015-7

5 Punkte

4. The following words have different meanings. Which of the meanings below is the one used in the text on page 5? Tick (✓) the correct meaning. There is an example at the beginning (0).

0. last (line 1)

✓ **letzte(r, s)** *(Adj.)*

☐ zuletzt *(Adv.)*

☐ dauern *(Verb ohne Obj.)*

☐ reichen *(Verb ohne Obj.)*

1. time (line 4)

☐ Zeit *(Nomen)*

☐ Mal *(Nomen)*

☐ stoppen *(Verb + Obj.)*

☐ einen geeigneten Zeitpunkt wählen *(Verb + Obj.)*

2. turn (line 22)

☐ wenden, umdrehen *(Verb + Obj.)*

☐ abbiegen *(Verb)*

☐ werden *(Verb ohne Obj.)*

☐ Kurve, Biegung *(Nomen)*

3. mean (line 26)

☐ bedeuten *(Verb + Obj.)*

☐ meinen *(Verb)*

☐ geizig *(Adj.)*

☐ gemein *(Adj.)*

4. light (line 31)

☐ Licht *(Nomen)*

☐ anzünden *(Verb + Obj.)*

☐ erleuchten *(Verb + Obj.)*

☐ leicht *(Adj.)*

5. like (line 35)

☐ mögen *(Verb + Obj.)*

☐ möchten *(Verb + Obj.)*

☐ wie *(Präp.)*

☐ also *(Adv.) (umgs)*

E 2015-8 / Qualifizierender Abschluss der Mittelschule – Englisch 2015

20 Punkte

D Text Production (Dictionary allowed)

Wähle eine Aufgabe:

I. Correspondence: **E-Mail**

oder

II. Creative Writing: **Picture Story**

I. **Correspondence:** E-Mail

Deine Schule veranstaltet im Rahmen eines Austauschprogramms mit Schottland eine Reise nach Inverness. Du nimmst daran teil. Ihr seid in Gastfamilien untergebracht und du wohnst bei Alex.

Schreibe eine E-Mail auf Englisch an Alex.

- Du freust dich auf die bevorstehende Reise im Juli.
- Du stellst dich vor und erzählst von dir, z. B. von der Schule, von Hobbys.
- Du hast noch zwei Fragen an Alex, und zwar jeweils eine
  – zur Klasse oder Schule bzw.
  – zu Hobbys oder Freizeitaktivitäten.
- Du erkundigst dich nach weiteren Punkten. Wähle zwei davon:
  – Besuch von Sehenswürdigkeiten oder vorgesehenen Ausflugszielen, z. B. Loch Ness
  – deine Unterbringung, z. B. eigenes Zimmer
  – mögliche Abendgestaltung
  – geeignete Kleidung
  – geplantes Programm
- Du informierst Alex noch über Wichtiges, z. B. über Allergien, Essgewohnheiten.

Schreibe eine E-Mail von ungefähr **12 Sätzen** bzw. etwa **100 Wörtern** auf ein extra Blatt. Denke an eine ansprechende äußere Form.

II. **Creative Writing:** Picture Story
Betrachte die Bilder und schreibe eine Geschichte auf Englisch.
Beginne wie folgt:

The Scottish castle ghost

Last summer Callum and his class visited …

Schreibe eine Geschichte von ungefähr **12 Sätzen** bzw. etwa **100 Wörtern** auf ein extra Blatt. Denke an eine ansprechende äußere Form.

Qualifizierender Abschluss der Mittelschule Bayern 2016
Englisch

E 2016-1

A Listening Comprehension (No dictionary allowed)

There are four parts to the test. You'll hear each part twice. At the end of each part you'll have some time to complete the tasks.

Task 1: Peter Thompson from the USA is calling the tourist office in Stratford, England.
There is <u>one mistake</u> in each sentence.
Listen and write down the correct information.
There is an example (0) at the beginning.

5 Punkte

William Shakespeare

0. I'm going on a holiday in Europe later ~~next~~ year.
   this

1. We're thinking about spending two or three weeks in Stratford.

   _____

2. There are even more tourists than usual.

   _____

3. William Shakespeare died in 1600.

   _____

4. You missed the great parade on 3rd April.

   _____

5. Find them on our website at shakespeareanniversary.com

   _____

Task 2: Peter Thompson and his son Robert have arrived in Stratford. They are on a sightseeing tour by bus.
Listen to the guide. Four of the statements (B–I) are <u>true</u>.
Write the letters in the box. There is an example (0) at the beginning.

4 Punkte

A **They have arrived at the Royal Shakespeare Theatre.**
B There you can see Shakespeare's plays on stage.
C The building is 170 years old.
D The theatre reopened in 2010.
E The Swan Theatre has about 500 seats.
F The ticket counters are open all day.
G One play by Shakespeare is currently in the programme.
H The tour will continue at 4.00.
I At the final stop they will visit Shakespeare's grave.

0	1	2	3	4
A				

E 2016-2 ✦ Qualifizierender Abschluss der Mittelschule – Englisch 2016

6 Punkte

Task 3: Robert Thompson is at the ticket counter of the Royal Shakespeare Theatre.

Listen to the conversation and fill in the missing information in the ticket reservation receipt. There is an example (0) at the beginning.

Royal Shakespeare Theatre
Ticket Reservation receipt: Robert Thompson

0. play: **Romeo and Juliet**

1. day of performance: _____

2. time of performance: _____

3. number of discount tickets: _____

4. price of tickets in total: £ _____

5. ticket pick-up time: until _____

6. seating: row _____

---

5 Punkte

Task 4: After the theatre, Robert (R) and his father (F) are at a local restaurant. What do they order?

Listen to the conversation and write *R* and *F* in the correct boxes of each list. There is an example (0) at the beginning.

0.
Drinks	
Coke	R
Fruit Juice	☐
Lemonade	☐
Mineral Water	F

1.
Starters	
Caesar's Salad	☐
French Pâté	☐
Tuna Salad	☐
Vegetable Soup	☐

2.
Main Course	
Grilled Fish	☐
Beef Steak	☐
Roast Beef	☐
Mixed Grill	☐

3.
Side orders	
Baked Potatoes	☐
Jacket Potatoes	☐
Mashed Potatoes	☐
Stuffed Potatoes	☐

4.
Side orders	
Cabbage	☐
Carrots	☐
Mushrooms	☐
Peas	☐

5.
Dessert	
Apple Pie	☐
Lemon Tart	☐
Toffee Ice-Cream	☐
Toffee Surprise	☐

| Qualifizierender Abschluss der Mittelschule – Englisch 2016 | E 2016-3 |

B Use of English (No dictionary allowed)

1. Breakfast

   10 Punkte

   Read the text. Fill in the gaps. Change the words given in the brackets to make them fit the sentences. There is an example (0) at the beginning.

   People have different ideas and (0 opinion) **opinions** about breakfast. Some people say it is the (1 important) _____ meal of the day. Statistics show that people who (2 not have) _____ breakfast often have problems with concentration and health. England is known for its cooked breakfast; but what (3 do) _____ this full English breakfast consist of? A typical English breakfast (4 include) _____ eggs, either poached or scrambled, with bacon and sausages, followed by toast with marmalade. A (5 health) _____ version is just one egg and some toast. Whereas in Europe, especially in Germany, people prefer (6 have) _____ cheese, ham, eggs and some bread as a start to the day, nearly all the southern (7 Europe) _____ countries tend to have only coffee and some bread or pastries. The tradition of the English breakfast (8 exist) _____ for many years, and visitors, hotel guests and people who have the time still enjoy it to this day. However, in our hectic and health-conscious world, many English people prefer a continental breakfast or they (9 quick) _____ get something to eat and drink on their way to work. It is likely that in future our culture of eating (10 change) _____ even more. The full English breakfast may soon be a thing of the past.

2. Tea

   10 Punkte

   Read the text and complete each sentence with <u>one</u> suitable word. There is an example (0) at the beginning.

   Since the 18th (0) **century** the United Kingdom has been one of the world's greatest tea consumers. At first, tea was mainly imported (1) _____ China. In those days it was sold in almost (2) _____ street in London. People at that time called it 'China drink'. Not only tea but also small porcelain tea cups were shipped to Europe. These cups were so thin that it was necessary to (3) _____ some milk in first, so that they (4) _____ not break when the hot tea went in. People still use these porcelain cups now and then for special occasions. Even today people in England add milk to their tea and some sugar, depending on their taste. In Britain the word 'tea' describes both a hot drink and a light meal in the afternoon (5) _____ about four o'clock. For some people it is their last meal of the day, for (6) _____ a snack between lunch and dinner. In many towns and cities in Britain there are tea rooms (7) _____ serve tea and other drinks. But since the 1950s many tea rooms (8) _____ closed. Today people prefer health-orientated drinks, for (9) _____ fruit or herbal teas. Nevertheless, (10) _____ is no other country in Europe where people drink more tea.

C Reading Comprehension (Dictionary allowed)

Fish and chips

Every country has a national dish, and for England, it's fish and chips.

A

1 Ahh ... freshly fried, hot fish and chips, with lots of salt and vinegar, wrapped in paper and eaten on a cold and wintry day – you simply cannot beat it! There is nothing more British than fish and chips. In 2010 *The Independent* newspaper wrote that the dish was more typical to England than the Queen or The Beatles. In Britain peo-
5 ple spend around £ 1.2 billion every year on fish and chips. In practically every village, town and city in England you can find at least one fish-and-chip shop, often affectionately called "the chippy".

B

As the name says, fish and chips is made of chips and a fish fillet which is dipped in batter and then deep-fried for a short time. Batter is a liquid mixture of flour, salt,
10 water and beer, which hardens when you fry it. Here is a great recipe for you to enjoy:

Ingredients:
- 3 cups of oil
- 2 large fish fillets
- 3 large potatoes

For the batter:
- 1 cup of flour (self-raising)
- ½ cup of sparkling water
- ½ teaspoon of salt
- 1 cup of beer

Cut your potatoes into small sticks. Boil the potatoes in water for 3 minutes. Place on a large oven tray and sprinkle some oil and a little salt on top. Bake at 250 °C for about 20–25 minutes.

Mix the ingredients for the batter in a bowl. Put the oil in a deep pan and start heating. Dip the fish into the batter and put it into the hot oil. Wait until the batter is golden and brown, usually 4–5 minutes.

C

The dish dates back as far as the 16th century, when the Spanish introduced the idea of frying the fish instead of boiling or cooking it. The first fish-and-chip shop probably opened in London in 1860. Fish and chips was a traditional dish on a Friday,
15 when the Catholic Church asked people not to eat meat – and, for some reason, fish was not meat for them. During the Second World War, fish and chips was one of the foods that were not rationed in England. Before, during, and even after the war, fish

Qualifizierender Abschluss der Mittelschule – Englisch 2016   ✦ E 2016-5

and chips remained popular, especially among poorer, working-class people because it was cheap and filling.

D

20 Today there are around 10,500 fish-and-chip shops across the UK, making British fish and chips the nation's favourite take-away. But fish and chips is no longer just fast food. You can find posh versions of it in the best restaurants up and down the country. It is a favourite for lunch, dinner or even after a night out. As soon as you have ordered your fish and chips in a chippy, you will get a lot of greasy chips, fol-
25 lowed by a hot and crispy piece of fish. Then the person behind the counter will ask, "salt and vinegar?" For most British people salt and vinegar is a must. Many people also like them with mushy peas and some even with curry sauce.

E

An English pop song reminds us that "yesterday's newspaper is tomorrow's chip paper". For many years fish and chips was traditionally sold wrapped in old news-
30 papers because the newspaper kept the food warm. Nowadays using newspaper is no longer allowed for health and safety reasons. To keep up the tradition, some chippies now use fake newspaper, while others use waxed paper. Less popular is the use of plastic because it is difficult to recycle.

F

British consumers eat some 382 million portions of fish and chips every year, but is
35 that good for them? Fish and chips contain fewer calories than pizza, burgers and other take-away options. They are a valuable source of protein, iron and vitamins. And last but not least: according to psychologist Dr David Lewis traditions are for adults what a comfort blanket is for a child. So fish and chips is a super meal which is both physically and mentally very satisfying.

Adapted from: www.historic-uk.com/CultureUK/Fish-Chips, www.federationoffishfriers.co.uk

1. Read the text on pages 4 and 5. Match the correct titles (1–8) to the para-   5 Punkte
graphs (B–F). Write the correct number in the boxes below. Use each number only once. There are three extra titles. There is an example (0) at the beginning.

   0̸ Fish and chips – a national symbol

   1   Fish and chips in other countries

   2   Packaging fish and chips

   3   A meal for many occasions and tastes

   4   Healthy for body and soul

   5   The price for a portion

   6   Historical facts

   7   How to prepare the dish

   8   Even the Queen likes fish and chips

paragraph A	paragraph B	paragraph C	paragraph D	paragraph E	paragraph F
0					

E 2016-6　Qualifizierender Abschluss der Mittelschule – Englisch 2016

5 Punkte

2. Answer the questions using information from the text on pages 4 and 5. Short answers are possible. There is an example (0) at the beginning.

　0. What is the nickname for a fish-and-chip shop?
　Chippy

　1. What four ingredients do you need for the batter?

　_____

　2. Who were the first to prepare fish in hot oil?

　_____

　3. Why did poorer people like fish and chips so much? Give <u>two</u> reasons.

　_____

　4. What was the reason for selling fish and chips in old newspapers?

　_____

　5. Which wrapping material is bad for the environment?

　_____

5 Punkte

3. Read the text on pages 4 and 5. Which part of the text gives you the following information? Write the number of the line or lines in the box. There is an example (0) at the beginning.

	line or lines
0. There are fish-and-chip shops everywhere in England.	**5–6**
1. Upper-class menus may also include fish and chips.	
2. The typical question of the chippy owner when you order	
3. There is a wrapping material that looks like newspaper.	
4. The number of fish-and-chip meals sold in Britain annually	
5. Certain substances in fish and chips are good for your body.	

| | Qualifizierender Abschluss der Mittelschule – Englisch 2016 | E 2016-7 |

4. Five of the statements (b–j) are <u>true</u>. Choose the five true statements according to the information given in the text on pages 4 and 5. Write the letters of the true statements on the lines below. There is an example (0) at the beginning.

5 Punkte

a	**Fish and chips is a real treat on a cold day in winter.**	*True statements:*
b	British fish-and-chip shops sell around 1.2 billion servings of fish and chips per year.	0. a
c	Before you fry the fish fillet you put it into a mixture called batter.	1. _____
d	You put the fish fillet on an oven tray and bake it for about 20–25 minutes.	2. _____
e	You need to fry the fish for about four to five minutes.	3. _____
f	The Church said that people shouldn't eat meat on Fridays, so they often had fish and chips instead.	4. _____
g	In World War II fish and chips weren't available.	5. _____
h	Fish and chips is no longer the most popular fast food in Britain.	
i	The British like eating fish and chips at different mealtimes and also after going out.	
j	Most of the popular fast foods have more calories than the British national dish.	

D   Text Production (Dictionary allowed)

20 Punkte

Wähle eine Aufgabe:

I. Correspondence: **E-Mail** oder II. Creative Writing: **Picture Story**

I. **Correspondence:** E-Mail
Du besuchst auf der Insel Malta einen Sprachkurs. Du denkst an deine spanischen Freunde, José und Carmen, die du letztes Jahr kennengelernt hast. Du schreibst an einen von beiden eine E-Mail auf Englisch.

- Erzähle, warum du auf Malta bist.
- Beschreibe deinen Aufenthalt und berichte z. B. über
  - Sprachkurs, Lehrkräfte, Mitstudenten
  - Unterkunft, Gastfamilie
  - Freizeitaktivitäten nach dem Sprachkurs oder am Wochenende
- Schildere einen Unterrichtstag und schreibe z. B. über
  - Anzahl der Stunden
  - Pausengestaltung
  - Mahlzeiten

- Frage, ob er/sie auch schon eine Sprachreise gemacht hat.
- Berichte über deinen Plan, im nächsten Sommer einen Folgekurs zu besuchen, und frage, ob er/sie dann mitkommen möchte.

Schreibe eine E-Mail von ungefähr **12 Sätzen** bzw. etwa **100 Wörtern** auf ein gesondertes Blatt. Achte auf eine ansprechende äußere Form.

II. **Creative Writing:** Picture Story
Betrachte die Bilder und schreibe eine Geschichte auf Englisch. Beginne wie folgt:

A new job
One morning, Mr Smith, the zoo director, and Nick, the zookeeper, were in a panic ...

Schreibe eine Geschichte von ungefähr **12 Sätzen** bzw. etwa **100 Wörtern** auf ein gesondertes Blatt. Achte auf eine ansprechende äußere Form.

| | | E 2017-1 |

Qualifizierender Abschluss der Mittelschule Bayern 2017
Englisch

A Listening Comprehension (No dictionary allowed)

There are four parts to the test. You'll hear each part twice. At the end of each part you'll have some time to complete the tasks.

Task 1: Kim is talking to her uncle Bob on the phone.
Listen to the dialogue and fill in the missing information.
There is an example (0) at the beginning.

5 Punkte

0. Kim wants to become a **car mechanic**.

1. Kim could do an apprenticeship at _____ Garage.

2. Kim must have good grades in _____ and _____.

3. Kim doesn't need work experience or a _____.

4. The garage is in _____.

5. David, the _____ mechanic, has more information about the job.

Task 2: David is talking about his work experience in his video blog.
Read the statements (B–I). Listen to David and find the four <u>true</u> statements.
Write the letters in the box. There is an example (0) at the beginning.

4 Punkte

A̶ **David worked in Australia for a while.**

B   He used to repair mobile phones.

C   People brought their cars to his garage.

D   He repaired the cars where they broke down.

E   All the parts he needed were in his truck.

F   He often had to work long hours.

G   Sometimes he even got wet when he was working.

H   He hates Australia because of the snakes and spiders.

I   He learned to be careful of dangerous animals.

0	1	2	3	4
A				

	Qualifizierender Abschluss der Mittelschule – Englisch 2017

6 Punkte

Task 3: Kim has a job interview at the garage. She is talking to the manager. Listen to the conversation and answer the questions. Write short answers. There is an example (0) at the beginning.

0. How old is Kim?
   16

1. When will she finish school?

   _____

2. Who showed her how to repair a car?

   _____

3. What makes the heavy work in a garage easier?

   _____

4. How much will she earn at the beginning?
   £ _____ a _____

5. When can Kim start the job?

   _____

6. When will Mr Brown call her?
   By _____

5 Punkte

Task 4: It's Kim's second day at the garage. She and Dave are talking to a customer. Listen to the conversation and fill in the missing details in the form. There is an example (0) at the beginning.

Order No.	127543
Date	27/06/2017
Customer's car	problem: **0. strange noise**
Rental car	☑ YES ☐ NO
Price	1. £ _____ per day including 200 miles & insurance
Car details and extras	automatic 2. _____

| Qualifizierender Abschluss der Mittelschule – Englisch 2017 | ⟋ E 2017-3 |

Fuel	type:
	3. _____
	Return with full tank or pay
	4. £ _____ extra
Import	Call customer
	5. after _____

B   Use of English (No dictionary allowed)

1. Martin, a German working in England, writes to his friend Julia.
    Read the text and complete each sentence with <u>one</u> suitable word.
    There is an example (0) at the beginning.

    7 Punkte

    Hello Julia,

    How are you? I (0) **am** writing to you from Birmingham. I'll be here (1)
    _____ the next two weeks. My company asked me (2) _____
    I was interested in working in Britain this summer. As you can imagine, I was
    more (3) _____ happy. I'm staying with a very nice family and the
    host father (4) _____ in the same factory. I am the only German here
    so I have to talk English all the time. I think my English (5) _____
    already improved quite a lot since I arrived here. I am really enjoying my stay
    and I love working here.
    When I'm back home I (6) _____ definitely recommend such a visit
    to my colleagues.
    I am looking forward to (7) _____ from you soon.

    Love,

    Martin

2. Julia answers Martin's e-mail.
    Read the text and complete it with words from the box. Use <u>one</u> word for
    each gap. There is an example (0) at the beginning.

    7 Punkte

    > about • abroad • at • because • book • but • by • during
    > from • more • much • over • real • spend • spent • that
    > there • these • where • whereas • while • will

    Dear Martin,

    What a pleasant surprise (0) **having** you here in Britain. Did all the trainees
    have the chance to work (1) _____ or did your company

E 2017-4 / Qualifizierender Abschluss der Mittelschule – Englisch 2017

choose you (2) _____ of your excellent results in your
exams? You have to tell me more about it.

I would love to see you (3) _____ you are here. I could come
to Birmingham next weekend so that we could (4) _____ some
time together. I could stay (5) _____ my aunt's. Have I ever
mentioned that my mum's sister and her family live in (6) _____
area? My cousin Jo told me about an amusement park which is interesting and
not far away. What do you think (7) _____ spending a day there?
Perhaps together with Jo? If you like my idea or if you have any other sugges-
tions, please write back soon, so we can fix a date.

Love,

Julia

6 Punkte 3. Read Martin's letter to his host family. There are six mistakes in the text.
Find them and write the correct word(s) on the numbered line.
There is an example (0) at the beginning.

Dear all,	
I arrived home safely after a pleasant flight,	
although the departure was delayed for <u>much</u>	**0. more**
than one hour. Unfortunately, my suitcase	
was not on the plane, but he was delivered to	1. _____
my house by the airline later. So I was able to	
give the presents to my family. My grandma	
love the teapot and especially the tea.	2. _____
My brother immediately put on the football	
shirt of the English national team and doesn't	3. _____
want to take it off again until he went to bed.	
My father and my sister liked her gifts, too.	4. _____
I am so grateful that you helped me to find	
souvenirs for everybody. My visit went by	
very quickly and I've already be back at work	5. _____
since five days, but I have so many pleasant	6. _____
memories of my stay in England.	
Best regards and thanks from my parents.	
Love,	
Martin	

Qualifizierender Abschluss der Mittelschule – Englisch 2017   ✦ E 2017-5

C Reading Comprehension (Dictionary allowed)

Amusement Parks

A

1 An amusement park or theme park is a group of entertainment attractions, rides, and other events in a large outdoor area, often covering many square kilometers. Amusement parks always stay at the same location, not like e. g. travelling funfairs, and they offer more than simple city parks or playgrounds.

B

5 Today's amusement parks have developed from a variety of influences. It all started with the fairs in the Middle Ages, which became places of entertainment for the masses with attractions like freak shows, acrobatics and juggling. Another influence were the English pleasure gardens, popular between 1550 and 1700. Originally they were entertainment areas just for rich people but soon everybody could enjoy their attrac-
10 tions e. g. fireworks, music, dancing and animal acrobatics. The Prater in Vienna, which opened at the end of the 18th century, served as an example which was copied by many amusement parks worldwide.

C

The amusement park industry offers large and world-famous theme parks but there are also smaller or medium-sized family fun parks, which sometimes started as minia-
15 ture golf courses and then grew to include go-karts, bumper cars, bumper boats, water slides and even roller coasters. There are also parks that use rides and attractions for educational purposes. Some parks focus on prehistoric animals showing dinosaurs in natural settings, while other parks offer several thousand animals, fish and other sea life and give information about them.

D

20 The greatest attractions of amusement parks are of course the rides. Classic rides are roller coasters, which usually include a steep drop from the highest point and a sharp curve taken at full speed. Water rides are especially popular in the summer when it is hot. Dark rides, e. g. ghost trains, are enclosed attractions which include animations, music and other special effects. The Ferris wheel is the most common type of amuse-
25 ment ride. In the big parks where the attractions are far apart, transport rides are used to take large numbers of guests from one area to another, as an alternative to walking.

E

Amusement parks get most of their money from admission fees. In amusement parks using the pay-as-you-go scheme a guest enters the park for free. The guest must then buy tickets for the rides at each attraction's entrance. An amusement park using the
30 pay-one-price scheme will charge guests one large admission fee. The guests are then entitled to use most of the attractions in the park as often as they wish during their visit. Parks also earn money with parking fees, food and beverage sales and souvenirs.

F

Amusement parks have come a long way since their beginnings and have always re-
flected the latest technology of their time. In order to attract customers they constantly
35 need to offer the latest and greatest rides. Let's have a look at the future of roller coasters for example. They are thrilling rides anyway but what if virtual-reality experiences
are added? Passengers wear mobile virtual reality headsets that present 3D adventures
while riding a coaster. So they can take a simulated journey aboard a flying dragon, a
rocket ship or some other fantasy scenario. Considering the speed with which society
40 and technology are changing, we can expect a lot of new attractions in amusement
parks around the world within the coming years.

Safety rules

Taking an amusement ride is one of the safest recreational activities.

Accidents do happen, however, but the reason for most accidents is rider misbehavior.

- Follow all posted height, age and medical restrictions; observe all rules and verbal
45 instructions issued by ride operators.
- Make sure the restraints fit well and you are secured in your seat.
- Double-check seat belts, shoulder harnesses and lap bars. Hold onto handrails when provided.
- Keep all body parts and belongings inside the ride at all times.
50 - Never stand up on a roller coaster to get a bigger thrill.
- If a ride stops temporarily, due to breakdown or other reason, stay seated and wait for the ride to start up again or for an operator to give you further instructions.
- Do not board a ride if it looks poorly maintained or if the operator is inattentive.
- Never ride while under the influence of alcohol or drugs.

5 Punkte

1. Read the text on pages 5 and 6.
   Match the titles (1–8) to the paragraphs (B–F). Write the correct number in the boxes below. Use each number only once. There are three extra titles. There is an example (0) at the beginning.

   Ø **Definition**

   1 Horse riding

   2 Earlier traditions

   3 Financial aspects

   4 New developments

   5 Attractions for students

   6 Different types of parks

   7 Activities in modern parks

   8 Accommodation for visitors

paragraph A	paragraph B	paragraph C	paragraph D	paragraph E	paragraph F
0					

5 Punkte

2. Answer the questions using information from the text on pages 5 and 6. Short answers are possible. There is an example (0) at the beginning.

   0. What is similar to an amusement park but changes its location?
   a travelling funfair

   1. Who were the only visitors when English pleasure gardens first opened?

   _____

   2. Which park became a model for a lot of other parks?

   _____

   3. What indoor attractions need very little light?

   _____

| Qualifizierender Abschluss der Mittelschule – Englisch 2017 | E 2017-7 |

4. Which system asks visitors to pay an entrance fee to the park?

_____

5. What device will add more excitement to roller-coaster rides in the future?

_____

3. The following words have different meanings. Which of the meanings below is the one used in the text on pages 5 and 6?
   Tick (✓) the correct meaning. There is an example (0) at the beginning.

   5 Punkte

   0. stay (line 3)
      - ☐ Aufenthalt *(Nomen)*
      - ✓ **bleiben** *(Verb)*
      - ☐ Besuch *(Nomen)*
      - ☐ stehen bleiben *(Verb)*

   1. focus (line 17)
      - ☐ Mittelpunkt *(Nomen)*
      - ☐ klar sehen *(Verb)*
      - ☐ Brennpunkt *(Nomen)*
      - ☐ sich konzentrieren *(Verb)*

   2. drop (line 21)
      - ☐ tropfen *(Verb)*
      - ☐ Tropfen *(Nomen)*
      - ☐ Fall *(Nomen)*
      - ☐ fallen lassen *(Verb)*

   3. mobile (line 37)
      - ☐ Handy *(Nomen)*
      - ☐ transportabel *(Adj.)*
      - ☐ Mobile *(Nomen)*
      - ☐ flexibel *(Adj.)*

   4. fit (line 46)
      - ☐ passen *(Verb)*
      - ☐ geeignet *(Adj.)*
      - ☐ Anfall *(Nomen)*
      - ☐ in Form *(Adj.)*

5. board (line 53)

☐ Brett *(Nomen)*

☐ Behörde *(Nomen)*

☐ einsteigen *(Verb)*

☐ verschlafen *(Verb)*

5 Punkte 4. Five of the statements (b–j) are <u>true</u>. Choose the true statements according to the information given in the text on pages 5 and 6. Write the letters of the true statements on the lines below. There is an example (0) at the beginning.

a	**Usually amusement parks are very large.**	*True statements:*
b	Only a few people came to the fairs in the Middle Ages.	**0. a**
c	Miniature golf courses usually include other attractions like go-karts or bumper cars.	1. _____
		2. _____
d	In some parks you can learn about creatures of the ocean.	3. _____
e	Water rides are the park visitors' favourite attraction all year round.	4. _____
f	Big parks offer their visitors an easy way to get around.	5. _____
g	Only nowadays amusement parks use the latest technology.	
h	Fast developing technology offers many possibilities for future park attractions.	
i	Check that you are old enough if you want to go on a ride.	
j	Don't get off a ride if it stops temporarily.	

Qualifizierender Abschluss der Mittelschule – Englisch 2017 | ⁄ E 2017-9

20 Punkte

D   Text Production (Dictionary allowed)

Wähle eine Aufgabe:

Correspondence: Application and CV

oder

Creative Writing: Picture and Prompts

Application and CV

Du suchst einen Ferienjob im Ausland und findest die Anzeige einer Agentur, die Ferienjobs in einem Freizeitpark vermittelt.

Du wendest dich auf Englisch an Herrn Johnson, den zuständigen Ansprechpartner, und schickst ihm ein Anschreiben und einen tabellarischen Lebenslauf.

1. Verfasse das Anschreiben und gehe auf folgende Inhaltspunkte ein:
   - Wo hast du die Anzeige gefunden?
   - Welchen Job möchtest du gerne im Freizeitpark ausüben?
   - Warum bist du dafür geeignet?
   - Warum interessiert dich ein Ferienjob im Ausland?
   - In welchem Zeitraum möchtest du arbeiten?
   - Erkundige dich nach Verpflegung und Unterkunft.
   - Verweise auf den Lebenslauf.

2. Verfasse den tabellarischen Lebenslauf mit folgenden Inhalten:
   - Persönliche Angaben
   - Schulbildung
   - Praktische Erfahrungen
   - Besondere Kenntnisse
   - Persönliche Interessen

Verfasse ein Anschreiben mit mindestens **80 Wörtern** auf ein gesondertes Blatt. Schreibe einen Lebenslauf von mindestens **30 Wörtern**. Verwende dazu eine eigene Seite.

Achte auf eine ansprechende äußere Form und eine gut lesbare Handschrift.

E 2017-10

Qualifizierender Abschluss der Mittelschule – Englisch 2017

Picture and Prompts

Schreibe eine Geschichte auf Englisch, in der du das Bild und die Angaben berücksichtigst.

Beginne wie folgt:

What a shock!
Last year Barbara took her English friend Megan to the Oktoberfest ...

| Fahrt mit dem Karussell | Gespräch | Missgeschick |

| Reaktion der Personen |

Schreibe eine Geschichte von mindestens **100 Wörtern** auf ein gesondertes Blatt. Achte auf eine ansprechende äußere Form und eine gut lesbare Handschrift.

Qualifizierender Abschluss der Mittelschule Bayern 2018 **Englisch**	✔ E 2018-1

A Listening Comprehension (No dictionary allowed)

There are three parts to the test. You'll hear each part twice.
At the end of each part you'll have some time to complete the tasks.

Task 1: Lauren and Toby, two teenagers from Calgary, are talking about their plans for the weekend. There is <u>one</u> mistake in each sentence below. Listen and write the correct information on the line. There is an example (0) at the beginning.

8 Punkte

0. I'm going ~~hiking~~ in the Rocky Mountains on Saturday. **rock-climbing**

1. I haven't been there since I was a baby.

   _____

2. I've even got a special ticket.

   _____

3. It's only 16 Canadian dollars and you can go as often as you like.

   _____

4. My younger brother's favorite animals are the crocodiles and the dolphins.

   _____

5. It had been closed for seven weeks because of repair work.

   _____

6. Some of the models were damaged by that horrible fire last October.

   _____

7. It'll be windy and cloudy on Saturday.

   _____

8. The zoo doesn't open at 10 on Sundays.

   _____

Task 2: On Sunday Lauren is waiting at the zoo entrance when Toby calls her. Listen to the telephone conversation and fill in the missing information. There is an example (0) at the beginning.

5 Punkte

0. Toby is already **10 minutes** late.

1. Toby has to take the C-train, line _____.

2. At the moment, there are no trains because of _____.

3. Toby will be at the zoo at about _____.

4. Toby's favorite animals are the _____.

5. They meet on the _____ in the middle of the zoo.

E 2018-2 ✦ Qualifizierender Abschluss der Mittelschule – Englisch 2018

7 Punkte

Task 3: Dave, the zookeeper at Calgary Zoo, is talking about Maska.
Listen and fill in the missing details. There is an example (0) at the beginning.

Maska

GENERAL INFORMATION

Native American name	• Maska
English meaning	• **(0) strong**
Weight	• (1) _____ kg
Top speed	• (2) _____ km/h
In the zoo	• since 2010

EARLY LIFE

Place of birth	• wilderness
Causing problems	• (3) seen near _____
	and in _____
	• (4) looking for _____

LIFE AT THE ZOO

Favorite toy	• red ball
He enjoys	• (5) _____
Regular food	• apples
	• oranges
	• (6) _____
	• nuts
	• fish
	• (7) meat, but only _____
Favorite food	• hard-boiled eggs

Bär: © Nagel Photography. Shutterstock

| | Qualifizierender Abschluss der Mittelschule – Englisch 2018 | E 2018-3 |

B Use of English (No dictionary allowed)

1. Read the text about railways in Canada. Find <u>seven</u> mistakes in the text and write the correct word on the numbered line. Write <u>only one word</u> to correct the mistake. There is an example (0) at the beginning.

7 Punkte

	correct word
In the early years the railway played a very important role in the development ~~about~~ Canada. Nowadays it is more and less used to transport goods. Bus tickets are cheaper as train tickets and planes are more popular if you are short of time. But when you take the time and travel with train, the experience of traveling will certainly be unforgettable. Lots of tourists drive the train through the Rocky Mountains and enjoy the incredible views of the landscape. Over the years the train has served many purposes. At the first half of the last century there used to be a wagon equipped with a classroom, a library and accommodation for a teacher. It traveled around the country every month and children which lived in remote areas was able to have at least two or three days' teaching each month before the train took the wagon to the next remote location.

0. of
1. _____
2. _____
3. _____
4. _____
5. _____
6. _____
7. _____

2. Read the text about whale watching. Fill in the gaps using the words in brackets. Change the words, if necessary, to make them fit the sentence. Do not change the text. There is an example (0) at the beginning.

7 Punkte

Watching whales is very popular with (0 *tourist*) **tourists**. Vancouver Island in West Canada is a (1 *good*) _____-known place for whale watching. Quite a few agencies offer such tours. And since the 1980s these tours (2 *be*) _____ increasingly popular among tourists. You can choose between a tour on a motor or a sailing boat. Or you can even book a helicopter tour. Of course, this is really expensive but it (3 *offer*) _____ a completely different perspective. On the boat tours you get very (4 *close*) _____ to the giants of the ocean. It is not dangerous because these animals are quite peaceful and never attack people. You could even paddle among them in a kayak. But this can be a bit risky because a whale's normal movements could (5 *easy*) _____ turn your kayak over. 'Swimming with the whales' would then be (6 *include*) _____ in the price! An experience you (7 *not forget*) _____ for the rest of your life. Vancouver Island is indeed worth a visit.

6 Punkte

3. Read the text about the Yukon Quest. Fill each gap with <u>one</u> word that fits the sentence. Do not change the text. There is an example (0) at the beginning.

The Yukon Quest is (0) **the** hardest dog-sled race in the world. To get from Whitehorse to Fairbanks, which is a distance of about 1,600 km or one thousand (1) _____, the fastest drivers need about eight days. Some sled drivers need a few days longer but every year (2) _____ are several who have to give up. Temperatures down to minus forty degrees and heavy winds (3) _____ this race a real challenge for the humans as well as for the dogs.

The first race (4) _____ place in February 1984. The name "Yukon Quest" goes back to the historical highway to the north. During the gold rush, about a hundred and fifty years (5) _____, the gold seekers used sleds like the ones the Inuit had. According to the race rules, participants in the Yukon Quest today (6) _____ to compete using similar dog sleds.

The race is very popular, even in Europe. In 2002, it was won by a European for the first time.

Qualifizierender Abschluss der Mittelschule – Englisch 2018 ✦ E 2018-5

C Reading Comprehension (Dictionary allowed)

THE WORLD'S BEST TEACHER

A

1 The Canadian Maggie MacDonnell, born in 1980, won last year's Global Teacher Prize as the world's best teacher for her work in Salluit, an Inuit village in northern Quebec.

B

Salluit is a small village in the Canadian Arctic and you can
5 only reach it by plane. About 1,300 people live here and in winter the temperature can fall to – 25 °C. And this remote settlement faces some serious social problems. When MacDonnell first arrived at her school in Salluit, she saw classrooms with broken chairs and desks, and graffiti. There were not even any books to work with. Many teachers had left the school in the middle
10 of the year suffering from stress. The school did not have a principal either; he had left his job after only six weeks. Salluit's teenagers often live in very poor conditions. MacDonnell says that the majority of her students do not even have a bedroom – they sleep on the sofa in the living room.

C

Maggie MacDonnell realized how serious these problems were and decided to do
15 something about them. She has even become a temporary foster mother, giving a home to some of her own students. Maggie has already produced promising results, not only among the schoolchildren. All of Salluit's residents benefit from her work. All of this work is more than anyone can do in regular hours, and Maggie MacDonnell spends a lot of her free time on school activities. She says: "I think as a teacher in a
20 small Arctic village your day never ends. The school doors may close – but the relationship with your students continues, as you all live in the same place."

D

Ms. MacDonnell also uses her school project work to deal with local social problems. She has, for example, set up a community kitchen. The students help to prepare healthy meals which they serve to people who need them. The project teaches the
25 students about cooking and healthy eating, and also provides a useful service to the community. Together with her students, Ms. MacDonnell has also opened a fitness center. The young people helped with everything from painting to assembling equipment. Now all the village's residents can use the center. It helps to relieve stress and has important benefits for everyone with health problems. The praise the students get
30 for this project helps to build up their self-confidence. In addition Ms. MacDonnell spends a lot of time as a coach for the Salluit Running Club and in 2016 seven Inuit teenagers traveled with her to Hawaii to run a half marathon.

E

The key to her success is that she has always tried to turn students from problems into solutions. "You have to connect on a person-to-person level," she says. When asked
35 about technology in the classroom, MacDonnell says that such products can support learning, maybe, for highly motivated students with digital access. But it is completely different for students who are struggling to understand their own culture. "How can an app manage behavior? How can an unhappy student expect help from a tablet?" she says.

F

⁴⁰ So Maggie MacDonnell, who has been working at her small school for seven years, won the Global Teacher Prize for changing the lives of her students and transforming her community. Three of her Inuit students went with her to Dubai, where she received the $ 1 million award. She was among ten finalists chosen from 20,000 nominations and applications from 179 countries. This prize, which is now in its fourth ⁴⁵ year, was set up by the Varkey Foundation to show the important role teachers play in society. The Canadian Prime Minister congratulated MacDonnell in a video message. "We are all proud of you," he said.

4 Punkte

1. Read the text on pages 5 and 6. Tick (✓) the correct option for each gap according to the text. There is an example (0) at the beginning.

   0. Salluit is a ... in northern Quebec.

      ☐ national park

      ☐ remote province

      ☐ big city

      ☑ **small village**

   1. In Salluit the climate is rough, sometimes the temperature ... −25 °C.

      ☐ is colder than

      ☐ goes below

      ☐ even reaches

      ☐ is less than

   2. The prize was handed over to Maggie MacDonnell in ...

      ☐ Quebec

      ☐ Hawaii

      ☐ Dubai

      ☐ Salluit

   3. The Global Teacher Prize has existed for ... years.

      ☐ two

      ☐ four

      ☐ seven

      ☐ ten

   4. The prize wants to show that teachers are ... for society.

      ☐ valuable

      ☐ expensive

      ☐ dangerous

      ☐ responsible

Qualifizierender Abschluss der Mittelschule – Englisch 2018   ◆ E 2018-7

2. Read the text on pages 5 and 6. Then decide in which paragraph (A–F) you   5 Punkte
    find the answer to the questions (1–5). You can use the letters (A–F) <u>more
    than once</u>. There is an example (0) at the beginning.

    In which paragraph do you get the information that . . .

    0. . . . Maggie MacDonnell did not have a director at her workplace   **B**
        in Salluit?

    1. . . . the students feel better because of the positive feedback they
        get?

    2. . . . some of Maggie's students live with her for a while?

    3. . . . many teachers from all over the world wanted to become the
        world's best teacher?

    4. . . . the furniture at her school was in need of repair?

    5. . . . a politician from her home country honored Maggie's
        success?

3. Read the text on pages 5 and 6. Answer the questions using information from   6 Punkte
    the text. Short answers are possible. There is an example (0) at the beginning.

    0. What is Maggie MacDonnell's year of birth?
        1980

    1. How can you get to Salluit?

        _____

    2. What teaching material was missing when Maggie came to Salluit?

        _____

    3. Where do most of Maggie's students spend their nights?

        _____

    4. Which other project, apart from the fitness center, did Maggie start?

        _____

    5. Who is allowed to use the fitness center?

        _____

    6. For which sporting event did she train some of the young people?

        _____

E 2018-8 / Qualifizierender Abschluss der Mittelschule – Englisch 2018

5 Punkte

4. The following words have different meanings. Which of the meanings below
   is the one used in the text on pages 5 and 6?
   Tick (✓) the correct meaning. There is an example (0) at the beginning.

   0. work (line 2)
      - [✓] **Arbeit** *(Nomen)*
      - [ ] arbeiten *(Verb)*
      - [ ] funktionieren *(Verb)*
      - [ ] gelingen *(Verb)*

   1. face (line 7)
      - [ ] Fassade *(Nomen)*
      - [ ] gegenüberstehen *(Verb)*
      - [ ] Gesicht *(Nomen)*
      - [ ] zeigen nach *(Verb)*

   2. end (line 20)
      - [ ] aufhören *(Verb)*
      - [ ] beenden *(Verb)*
      - [ ] Ende *(Nomen)*
      - [ ] Ziel *(Nomen)*

   3. service (line 25)
      - [ ] Bedienung *(Nomen)*
      - [ ] Dienstleistung *(Nomen)*
      - [ ] instand halten *(Verb)*
      - [ ] Wartung *(Nomen)*

   4. spend (line 31)
      - [ ] Ausgabe *(Nomen)*
      - [ ] ausgeben *(Verb)*
      - [ ] verbrauchen *(Verb)*
      - [ ] verbringen *(Verb)*

   5. level (line 34)
      - [ ] eben *(Adjektiv)*
      - [ ] Ebene *(Nomen)*
      - [ ] gleichmachen *(Verb)*
      - [ ] Pegel *(Nomen)*

Qualifizierender Abschluss der Mittelschule – Englisch 2018 | E 2018-9

20 Punkte

D Text Production (Dictionary allowed)

Wähle eine Aufgabe:

Correspondence: Letter

oder

Creative Writing: Picture Story

Letter

Du hast dich bei einer Organisation, die internationale Brieffreundschaften vermittelt, angemeldet und erhältst nun Post von Sam aus Kanada.

- Antworte ihm auf Englisch und gehe dabei auf seinen Brief ein.
- Stelle ihm auch Fragen, z. B. zum Schulalltag in Kanada.

---

30 Apr 2018

Hi there,

I'm Sam (16), from Kelowna, British Columbia in Canada.
A few weeks ago I registered at the same international pen friend
organization as you did and got your address from them.

I'd like to hear more about you.
Please tell me about where you live, especially about Bavaria, your
interests, and your plans for the future.

And why do you want a pen friend from Canada?

Hope to hear from you soon.
Bye for now,

Sam

Verfasse einen Antwortbrief mit mindestens 100 Wörtern auf einem gesonderten Blatt.
Achte auf eine ansprechende äußere Form und eine gut lesbare Handschrift.

Picture Story

Schreibe eine Geschichte auf Englisch, in der du die Bilder berücksichtigst.

Beginne wie folgt:

A hungry squirrel
One day in winter Katie and her brother Jim were ...

Schreibe eine Geschichte von mindestens 100 Wörtern auf ein gesondertes Blatt. Achte auf eine ansprechende äußere Form und eine gut lesbare Handschrift.

Qualifizierender Abschluss der Mittelschule Bayern 2019
Englisch

E 2019-1

A Listening Comprehension (No dictionary allowed)

Task 1: Marcus and Laura are planning a holiday in London. Marcus has found a hotel on the internet. Now he is phoning the hotel to ask about rooms.
Fill in the missing information. There is an example (0) at the beginning.

6 Punkte

0. Laura and Marcus want to come to London at the **end** of August.

1. Laura and Marcus want to come to London on August _____.

2. They want to stay at the Portobello Hotel for two _____.

3. A double room costs £ _____ in summer.

4. The hotel is five minutes _____ from the tube station Holland Park.

5. From Holland Park it's six _____ to Oxford Circus.

6. Laura and Marcus are leaving on August _____.

Task 2: Marcus and Laura have gone to the London Visitor Centre. They want to find out about getting a London Pass.
There is one mistake in each sentence. Cross out the wrong word.
There is an example (0) at the beginning.

5 Punkte

0. We've ~~read~~ about something called a London Pass.

1. It gets you into terrific attractions in London.

2. And the best thing is that you don't have to queue to get in.

3. So if you don't pick up your card until late in the evening …

4. And can you get one here?

5. So we could order it now and pick it up tomorrow at 11?

Task 3: Marcus is talking to the receptionist at the hotel.
Answer the questions. Write short answers.
There is an example (0) at the beginning.

2 Punkte

0. How does Marcus want to go sightseeing?
   by tube

1. Which line does the receptionist think is better?
   the _____

2. How long does it take to walk from Bank station to the Tower?
   about _____

E 2019-2 Qualifizierender Abschluss der Mittelschule – Englisch 2019

7 Punkte

Task 4: Marcus and Laura are having breakfast at the hotel. They get into conversation with another guest. Are the sentences true (T) or false (F)? Tick (✓) the correct box. There is an example (0) at the beginning.

		T	F
0.	It is Marcus and Laura's first day in London.	☐	✓
1.	The guest arrived at the hotel this morning.	☐	☐
2.	The guest wants to stay in London for a week.	☐	☐
3.	The guest knows the main sights in London well.	☐	☐
4.	All museums in London are free.	☐	☐
5.	The British Museum is the most famous museum in London.	☐	☐
6.	This morning the guest wants to go to St Paul's Cathedral.	☐	☐
7.	Laura and Marcus travel home by plane.	☐	☐

B Use of English (No dictionary allowed)

4 Punkte

1. A famous singer
   Fill in the missing words. There is an example (0) at the beginning.

   The US rock singer Gwen Stefani was born (0) **in** Orange County, California (1) _____ October 3rd, 1969. She has got three brothers and sisters and they are all good (2) _____ music. Eric, one of Gwen's brothers, started the band called *No Doubt*.
   Gwen became the band's lead singer (3) _____ she was only 18. In 1995 Eric left the band because he got a job (4) _____ a cartoon artist.

4 Punkte

2. Travelling
   Write the word that matches the definition.
   There is an example (0) at the beginning.

   0. This person checks your ticket on the train.   **c o n d u c t o r**

   1. The building where trains stop so you
      can get on and off the trains   s _ _ _ _ _ _

   2. A ticket from London to Brighton
      and back again   r _ _ _ _ _ ticket

   3. A train that doesn't arrive on time is   l _ _ _ .

   4. A person who travels on a train, bus,
      ship or plane is called a   p _ _ _ _ _ _ _ _ .

4 Punkte

3. At the seaside
   Choose the correct word from the box.
   There is an example (0) at the beginning.

| Qualifizierender Abschluss der Mittelschule – Englisch 2019 | ✦ E 2019-3 |

| anyone • anything • anywhere • ~~everyone~~ • everywhere • someone • something • somewhere |

Susan and Tim went surfing with some friends and (0) **everyone** had a lot of fun. Suddenly Susan couldn't see Tim (1) _____. She looked for him (2) _____. Then she saw him at a hamburger stall. He was buying (3) _____ to eat because he hadn't had (4) _____ for breakfast.

4. Summer activities
   Fill in the right form of the verb. There is an example (0) at the beginning.

   4 Punkte

   Brenda (0 *be*) **is** a member of a youth club. Every year the club (1 *offer*) _____ summer activities.

   At the moment Brenda and her friends are sitting on the train to Brighton. A friendly lady starts talking to them. She asks Brenda, "(2 *be*) _____ you ever _____ to Brighton?"

   Brenda answers, "Unfortunately not. It's my first time. Last year I was on holiday near Brighton but I (3 *not go*) _____ to Brighton itself. So this time I (4 *want*) _____ to do some sightseeing."

5. Chris and Alex are talking about Alex's holiday
   Read the parts 1–5 and match them with one of the parts A–H. Write the letter in the correct box. There is an example (0) at the beginning and an example (5) at the end. You don't need all of Alex's statements.

   4 Punkte

	Chris
0	Hi, Alex. How are you?
1	Great. What was your holiday like?
2	Sounds fantastic. Did you spend a lot of money?
3	What places did you visit?
4	Oh, you're not? I love to go to interesting places. Were there any?
5	Sounds great. Maybe I should go there one day, too.

	Alex
A	Don't ask.
B	Yes, the flight was expensive, but the hotel was cheap.
C	Fine, thanks. What about you?
D	Everything was terrific – the beach, the weather, the hotel.
E	Of course there were. There were lots of things to see there.
F	I'm not really interested in sightseeing. I spent most of the time on the beach.
G	Yes, that's right. But the other things are good, too.
H	Good idea.

0	1	2	3	4	5
C					H

C Reading Comprehension (Dictionary allowed)

The London Eye

© SpaceKris. Shutterstock

1 Moving slowly, the capsule comes in from the left. Its doors open and you step in with about twenty other passengers. The doors close and the slow climb be-
5 gins. As you go up, you see one famous building after another across London. To the east St Paul's Cathedral, to the west Buckingham Palace, to the north the Telecom Tower. It's a breathtaking
10 spectacle, so breathtaking in fact that you haven't got time to be scared. Before you know it, you're 135 metres above one of Europe's most fascinating cities. Below you the Thames flows past the Houses of Parliament and Big Ben. If the weather is clear, you'll be able to see Windsor Castle, 38 km
15 away.

Then your ears pop and you're back in reality. You're standing in a glass capsule. From here cars, buses and taxis look like children's toys. But the ground is getting nearer and half an hour after boarding the London Eye you're leaving it. The "flight" was so exciting that you wish that you could get back on again immediately.

20 It's an easy ride, but planning and building the largest observation wheel in the world was not so easy. It was a huge project that took seven years. Over 1,700 people from five countries worked on it. "It was like building the pyramids in Egypt," says architect David Marks. "Parts were transported from France, the Czech Republic, Holland, Germany and Italy." In October 1999 the completed wheel was lifted above Britain's capi-
25 tal city.

The London Eye has been welcoming passengers since March 2000. It was a success from the beginning. In its first year British Airways had hoped for more than two million visitors. But three and a half million people came. Since then the numbers have stayed much the same. On busy summer days around 15,000 visitors take a flight. For
30 birthdays and other occasions you can hire a private capsule with buffet. At Christmas time you can even book a flight with wine and champagne. And for around £ 2,000 you can celebrate your wedding in a private capsule decorated with flowers.

Because of its spectacular location people have used the London Eye for demonstrations. In September 2004, for example, a man who called himself "Spiderman" climb-
35 ed to the top of the wheel. He was fighting for fathers' rights. His former partner had not allowed him to visit his four-year-old daughter.

Many years ago the London Eye was the highest observation wheel in the world. Today there is a much higher one in China. In London, it was more a question of vision than of size. "Our aim," explains David Marks, "was to create an exciting new way to see
40 and understand one of the greatest cities on earth."

Qualifizierender Abschluss der Mittelschule – Englisch 2019 ✏ E 2019-5

1. Read the text and choose the right title (A–G) for each paragraph of the text. — 5 Punkte
   Use each letter only once.
   One title (C) is already matched. There is one extra title.

   A. Difficulties in constructing the wheel

   B. Platform for protests

   C̶. Spectacular view of London sights

   D. Too expensive for tourists

   E. Similar attraction outside Europe

   F. Special offers for special events

   G. A short but exciting experience

lines 1–15	lines 16–19	lines 20–25	lines 26–32	lines 33–36	lines 37–40
C					

2. Are the sentences true (T) or false (F) or not in the text (N)? — 4 Punkte
   Tick (✓) the correct box.
   There is an example (0) at the beginning.

		T	F	N
0.	The capsule comes in from the right.	☐	✓	☐
1.	The London Eye moves very fast.	☐	☐	☐
2.	Building the London Eye was finished before the year 2000.	☐	☐	☐
3.	A man was arrested after his protest in 2004.	☐	☐	☐
4.	The London Eye is still the highest observation wheel in the world.	☐	☐	☐

3. Answer the questions using information from the text. Write <u>short</u> answers. — 6 Punkte
   There is an example (0) at the beginning.

   0. What's the height of the London Eye?
      135 metres

   1. How long does the 'flight' on the London Eye take?
      _____

   2. How long did it take to build the London Eye?
      _____

   3. When could the first passengers go on the London Eye?
      _____

   4. How many people go on the London Eye on a busy day?
      _____

5. What kind of events can you book a private capsule for?
Give **two** examples from the text.

_____

_____

5 Punkte

4. Write down the **complete** sentence from the text.
There is an example (0) at the beginning.

Which sentence tells you ...

0. that a larger group of people can ride in a capsule?
Its doors open and you step in with about twenty passengers.

1. that you can see very far from the London Eye?

_____

_____

_____

2. that from the top of the London Eye vehicles look very small?

_____

_____

3. that a lot of people from different countries helped to build the London Eye?

_____

_____

_____

4. how many people actually visited the London Eye within the first 12 months?

_____

_____

_____

5. that it's expensive if you want to have a wedding party on the London Eye?

_____

_____

_____

| Qualifizierender Abschluss der Mittelschule – Englisch 2019 | E 2019-7 |

D Text Production (Dictionary allowed)

20 Punkte

Wähle eine Aufgabe:

Correspondence: Email

oder

Creative Writing: Picture and prompts

Email

Im Urlaub warst du mit deinen Eltern im „Rainbow Hotel" in London. Nach eurer Rückkehr bemerkt ihr, dass ihr dort eine Reisetasche vergessen habt. Deine Eltern bitten dich, eine E-Mail auf Englisch an das Hotel zu schicken.

- Berichte, dass du bis gestern mit deinen Eltern in dem Hotel warst.
- Sage, dass euch der Aufenthalt dort gut gefallen hat.
- Erkläre, dass ihr eine Reisetasche im Zimmer vergessen habt.
- Mache Angaben über Stockwerk und Zimmernummer.
- Mache Angaben über den Ort, wo die Tasche sein könnte.
- Beschreibe die Tasche näher.
- Beschreibe den Inhalt der Tasche möglichst ausführlich.
- Bitte höflich darum, dass man euch die Tasche nachschickt.
- Verweise auf eure Postanschrift am Ende der E-Mail.
- Sage, dass ihr selbstverständlich die Versandkosten übernehmt.
- Bitte um baldige Beantwortung der E-Mail.

Schreibe eine E-Mail von ungefähr **100 Wörtern** auf ein gesondertes Blatt. Achte auf eine ansprechende äußere Form und eine gut lesbare Handschrift.

E 2019-8

Qualifizierender Abschluss der Mittelschule – Englisch 2019

Picture and prompts

Schreibe eine Geschichte auf Englisch, in der du das Bild und die Angaben berücksichtigst.

Beginne wie folgt:

Lost and found
Last Saturday afternoon Paul and Jake were in a games shop. Suddenly Jake saw a wallet ...

| Überraschung über Fund | Gedanken | Gespräch |

| Gemeinsame Entscheidung | Vorgang an der Kasse | Schluss |

Schreibe eine Geschichte von ungefähr **100 Wörtern** auf ein gesondertes Blatt. Achte auf eine ansprechende äußere Form und eine gut lesbare Handschrift.

Qualifizierender Abschluss der Mittelschule Bayern 2020
Englisch

E 2020-1

A Listening Comprehension (No dictionary allowed)

7 Punkte

Task 1: Anna and Ben are on their way to Melbourne. They are talking to Steve, another passenger on the plane.
Listen to the conversation and fill in the missing information.
There is an example (0) at the beginning.

Anna and Ben will soon arrive in Melbourne after a long (0) **flight**. They have come to Australia to learn how to (1) _____. They are going to do a 5-day beginners' course, which starts on (2) _____. But first they are going to spend three nights in Melbourne. Steve tells them to visit Skydeck, a (3) _____ platform at the top of a skyscraper. He says it is open almost all day, but the best time of day to go there is (4) _____. He warns them not to go there if they are afraid of heights because the platform has a (5) _____. When Anna and Ben ask about Phillip Island, where the penguins live, Steve tells them that it is 80 kilometres (6) _____ of Melbourne but there is a (7) _____ every hour and it is well worth a visit. Ben and Anna decide to visit Phillip Island the next day.

Task 2: Ben and Anna are on their way to Phillip Island. Listen to the guide and answer the questions.
There is an example (0) at the beginning.

6 Punkte

0. What kind of animals live on Phillip Island?
   the world's smallest penguins

1. How much of their time do the penguins spend in the ocean?
   _____ per cent of their time

2. What happens if visitors get too close to the penguins?
   _____

3. What can damage the eyes of the penguins?
   _____

4. What does the Penguin Foundation do? Give <u>one</u> example.
   _____

5. How much does it cost to adopt a penguin?
   $ _____ a year

6. How long will the viewing areas be open before the penguins arrive?
   _____

E 2020-2   Qualifizierender Abschluss der Mittelschule – Englisch 2020

7 Punkte

Task 3: On their last day in Melbourne, Ben and Anna are talking to the receptionist at their hotel. He gives them information about Melbourne Cricket Ground.

Listen and fill in the missing details. There is an example (0) at the beginning.

Melbourne Cricket Ground	
General Information	
seats sports	• (0) **100,000** • cricket • (1) _____ • Australian Football
Richmond Tigers – Today's Match	
against starts at	• (2) _____ • (3) _____
Guided Tour	
includes on match days	• (4) player's _____ • walk on the field • (5) no _____ tours
How to get there	
by bus on foot	• line 14 eastbound • (6) 10-minute _____ from the city centre
Tickets	
available	• at ticket counter • (7) on website: _____

B Use of English (No dictionary allowed)

7 Punkte

1. Read the following text about a camel ride. Fill in the gaps using the words in brackets. Change the words to make them fit the sentence.
   <u>Do not change the text</u>. There is an example (0) at the beginning.

   Like many other (0 *tour*) **tourists** in Australia, I went on a trip to Alice Springs. There I (1 *take*) _____ the opportunity to ride a camel. I was (2 *surprise*) _____ to learn that there were camels in Australia but actually it has the (3 *large*) _____ population of wild camels in the world. Someone who (4 *never ride*) _____ a camel before, may not know that the rider (5 *sit*) _____ much higher up than on a horse.

Qualifizierender Abschluss der Mittelschule – Englisch 2020   ✔ E 2020-3

Although camels usually move (6 *slow*) _____, they can also go faster than you might expect and then the rider is thrown backwards and forwards in the saddle.

I (7 *not feel*) _____ bad on the back of my camel yesterday; it is an experience that I can recommend to everyone.

2. Read the following text about surfing in Australia. Fill each gap with <u>one</u> suitable word. <u>Do not change the text</u>. There is an example (0) at the beginning.

      6 Punkte

   I've just arrived at the east coast (0) **where** impressive waves come crashing onto the beaches. Surfing is a very popular sport that has (1) _____ origins in Hawaii and which first came to Australia in 1915. Nowadays enthusiastic surfers (2) _____ around the world come to Australia (3) _____ the 50,000 km-long coast offers brilliant surfing waves. The oldest surfing competition in the world takes (4) _____ at Freshwater Beach and attracts over 7,000 competitors.

   A lot of Australians start surfing (5) _____ a very young age, and tomorrow I (6) _____ try it, too. I'm really looking forward to it.

3. Read the following text about the Sydney Hobart Race. Find <u>seven</u> mistakes in the text and write the correct word on the numbered line. Write <u>only one word</u> to correct the mistake.

      7 Punkte

   There is an example (0) at the beginning.

The race is one **in** the world's most difficult ocean races and traditionally start on 26th December. Hundreds of sailors come to Sydney all year. They sailed down Australia's east coast to Hobart in Tasmania. In 1945, when the race was first held, boats needed six and one half days to cover the 1,200 kilometres; today the record is under one day and ten hours. The start in Sydney is one of the Australian top event and lots of people come to the harbour to see the start. The race is very hard while weather conditions can be very dangerous. A number of boats and experienced sportsman have been lost during this race.	correct word
	(0) **of**
	(1) _____
	(2) _____
	(3) _____
	(4) _____
	(5) _____
	(6) _____
	(7) _____

C Reading Comprehension (Dictionary allowed)

Plogging – A 'Rubbish' way to get fit

The eco-friendly workout trend that is sweeping the globe has arrived in Australia.

A Is Sweden only famous for Vikings, reindeer and meatballs? Absolutely not! The latest Nordic trend is 'plogging', a new workout that has made it possible to get fit and to care for the environment at the same time. The word is a combination of 'jogging' and 'plocka' – the Swedish word for 'collecting'. But what exactly do the joggers collect? Well, they carry a bag with them, and whenever they spot a bottle, cup or any other litter, they stop for a second to pick up the rubbish and put it in their bag.

B The Swedish environmentalist Erik Ahlström started the plogging movement in 2016. After moving to Stockholm from a small ski-community in northern Sweden, Ahlström became angry about the amount of litter he saw along his cycle route to work every day. He explained, "The same trash would remain in the road for several weeks without anyone picking it up, so I started picking it up myself. It felt good in my heart to clean up even a small place." At first, he stopped occasionally to pick up trash, then it became part of his exercise routine.

C Since 2016 more and more people have followed his example. 'Plogging runs', with groups of people coming together to run and pick up trash in places like beaches or parks, have become popular events in Sweden. Since then the movement has spread around the world, mainly thanks to social media. Posts and hashtags, first used for organizing plogging events, have carried the activity from country to country because ploggers post images of themselves on social media proudly holding waste bags full of rubbish at the end of a run. Now over 40 countries are part of the official online 'Plogga' group and big events have taken place in nearly all of them. Although plogging started in Europe, plogging groups can now be found as far away as Ecuador, Thailand and even Australia. This worldwide success is far greater than the Swedish founder ever expected.

D Plogging is healthier than just jogging. According to Ahlström, half an hour of plogging burns 288 calories, compared with the 235 calories burned when simply jogging. When you run and stop repeatedly to pick up rubbish your pulse rate will go up and down, improving fat loss and fitness. Picking up litter uses muscles which don't get any training when you just go for a jog. Ahlström believes that the multiple benefits of plogging are what have helped make it so popular. "It's good for the body, good for the mind and, of course, good for the environment at the same time."

E In Ahlström's opinion, plogging is also popular because it is so simple. Unlike many other exercise trends, it doesn't require instruction or expensive equipment. "Everyone is allowed to do it in the way they want to," he says. You just need a bag, gloves and a suitable place to dispose of the rubbish afterwards. Many ploggers even take the litter home for recycling to make sure it doesn't end up as waste in the environment. Plastic, for example, decomposes extremely slowly and has deadly consequences for our wildlife.

F In the Pacific Ocean there is already a collection of plastic rubbish which covers an area as big as New South Wales and there will probably be three times more plastic waste in the world's oceans in the next 10 years. So, it's no surprise fitness fans are encouraging Australians to follow the Scandinavian example. Many ploggers take part in the 'Clean Up Australia Day' on the first Sunday of March each year. On this day last

Qualifizierender Abschluss der Mittelschule – Englisch 2020   E 2020-5

year, ploggers and others collected 6,400 tons of litter. Almost 40 per cent of this rub-
50 bish was made up of plastic items including bottles, bags, chip and chocolate wrappers.
By combining fitness and good housekeeping, we can stop rubbish from filling our
streets, beaches and parks and, in this way, save our most valuable asset: nature.
"When the rubbish is gone, nature can carry on."

1. Read the text on pages 4 and 5. Then decide in which paragraph (A–F) you   5 Punkte
   find the answer to each question (1–5). You can use any letter more than
   once. You do not need all the letters.
   There is an example (0) at the beginning.

   Which paragraph tells the reader that . . .

   0. the term plogging has its origins in different languages?
   1. you can start plogging without spending money or taking courses?
   2. people share pictures of themselves and the litter they have collected?
   3. in the future there will be a lot more plastic in the sea?
   4. it was just one person who had the idea of collecting rubbish while
      jogging?
   5. Erik Ahlström never thought that his movement would be such an inter-
      national hit?

0	1	2	3	4	5
A					

2. Answer the questions using information from the text on pages 4 and 5.   5 Punkte
   Short answers are possible. There is an example (0) at the beginning.

   0. What does 'plocka' mean in English?
      collecting

   1. How did Erik Ahlström usually get to work?

   _____

   2. Why is plogging healthier than jogging? Give <u>two</u> examples.

   _____

   _____

   3. How do ploggers keep their hands clean?

   _____

   4. What characteristic of plastic makes it a serious problem for nature?

   _____

   5. How much litter did ploggers pick up at one special event in Australia?

   _____

E 2020-6 | Qualifizierender Abschluss der Mittelschule – Englisch 2020

5 Punkte

3. Read the text on pages 4 and 5 and the statements (a–j). Five of the statements are <u>true</u>. Choose the true statements according to the information given in the text. Write the letters of the true statements on the lines below.
There is an example (0) at the beginning.

True statements
(0) **a**
(1) _____
(2) _____
(3) _____
(4) _____
(5) _____

a   Ploggers take a bag with them when they go jogging.

b   Ahlström has lived in Stockholm all his life.

c   For a long time, nobody removed the litter that Ahlström saw on his way to work.

d   It took some time until Ahlström combined jogging with picking up litter.

e   People in Sweden were not interested in 'plogging runs'.

f   Almost 40 countries belong to the 'Plogga' group.

g   Jogging burns fewer calories than plogging.

h   Plogging is popular although it is quite complicated.

i   'Clean Up Australia Day' takes place once a year.

j   Nearly forty per cent of the rubbish collected on 'Clean Up Australia Day' was plastic.

5 Punkte

4. The following words have different meanings. Which of the meanings below is the one used in the text on pages 4 and 5? Tick (✓) the correct meaning.
There is an example (0) at the beginning.

0. care (line 4)
- ☐ Sorgfalt *(Nomen)*
- ☐ Pflege *(Nomen)*
- ☑ **sich kümmern (Verb)**
- ☐ jmd. mögen *(Verb)*

1. spot (line 9)
- ☐ Fleck *(Nomen)*
- ☐ Ort *(Nomen)*
- ☐ etw. entdecken *(Verb)*
- ☐ etw. herausfinden *(Verb)*

2. spread (line 21)
- ☐ sich ausbreiten *(Verb)*
- ☐ Ausdehnung *(Nomen)*
- ☐ Umfang *(Nomen)*
- ☐ streichen *(Verb)*

3. stop (line 32)
- ☐ aufhören *(Verb)*
- ☐ stehenbleiben *(Verb)*
- ☐ Haltestelle *(Nomen)*
- ☐ beenden *(Verb)*

4. way (line 39)
- ☐ Art und Weise *(Nomen)*
- ☐ Weg *(Nomen)*
- ☐ Richtung *(Nomen)*
- ☐ Straße *(Nomen)*

5. waste (line 46)
- ☐ verschwenden *(Verb)*
- ☐ überflüssig *(Adj.)*
- ☐ Abfall *(Nomen)*
- ☐ Verschwendung *(Nomen)*

| Qualifizierender Abschluss der Mittelschule – Englisch 2020 | E 2020-7 |

D   Text Production (Dictionary allowed)   20 Punkte

Wähle eine Aufgabe:

Correspondence: E-mail

oder

Creative Writing: Picture story

E-mail

Deine Eltern haben euren Urlaub in einem Hotel gebucht. Die Buchung wurde mit der Buchungsnummer XRN23125 bestätigt und allgemeine Informationen zum Urlaubsort habt ihr bereits erhalten. Nun gibt es Änderungen in der Planung.

Du schreibst eine E-Mail an das Hotel auf Englisch.

- Schreibe, dass deine Eltern Zimmer gebucht haben und gib zunächst die Buchungsnummer an.
- Bedanke dich für die Bestätigung und die Informationen im Anhang.
- Teile mit, dass nun eine Person mehr mitkommt.
- Erkundige dich,
  - ob ein Einzelzimmer oder ein zusätzliches Bett möglich ist.
  - welche Kosten entstehen.
- Informiere das Hotel, dass ihr erst sehr spät anreist.
- Frage, wie ihr nach 22:00 Uhr an den Schlüssel kommt.
- Reserviere außerdem einen Parkplatz.
- Bitte darum, deine Anfrage bald zu beantworten.

Schreibe eine E-Mail von ungefähr **100 Wörtern** auf ein gesondertes Blatt. Achte auf eine ansprechende äußere Form und eine gut lesbare Handschrift.

Picture story

Schreibe eine Geschichte auf Englisch, in der du alle Bilder berücksichtigst.

Beginne wie folgt:

The lost key
Last Summer Trevor and his girlfriend ...

Schreibe eine Geschichte von ungefähr **100 Wörtern** auf ein gesondertes Blatt. Achte auf eine ansprechende äußere Form und eine gut lesbare Handschrift.

Qualifizierender Abschluss der Mittelschule Bayern 2021
Englisch

E 2021-1

Das Corona-Virus hat auch im vergangenen Schuljahr die Prüfungsabläufe beeinflusst. Um dir die Prüfung 2021 schnellstmöglich zur Verfügung stellen zu können, bringen wir sie in digitaler Form heraus.
Sobald die Original-Prüfungsaufgaben 2021 zur Veröffentlichung freigegeben sind, können sie als PDF auf der Plattform **MyStark** heruntergeladen werden (Zugangscode vgl. Farbseiten vorne im Buch).

Prüfung 2021

www.stark-verlag.de/mystark